BANHAM IN BUFFALO

5 YEARS OF THE PETER REYNER BANHAM FELLOWSHIP AT THE UNIVERSITY AT BUFFALO DEPARTMENT OF ARCHITECTURE

ORO EDITIONS
PUBLISHERS OF ARCHITECTURE, ART, AND DESIGN
GORDON GOFF: PUBLISHER
WWW.OROEDITIONS.COM
INFO@OROEDITIONS.COM

ISBN: 978-0-9826226-7-4

GRAPHIC DESIGN: **BRETT TABOLT**
PRODUCTION MANAGER: **USANA SHADDAY**
PRODUCTION ASSISTANT: **GABRIEL ELY**
PROJECT COORDINATOR: **CHRISTY LAFAVER**
EDITED BY: **MEHRDAD HADIGHI**
TEXT: **MEHRDAD HADIGHI, JONATHAN SOLOMON, SERGIO LOPEZ-PIÑEIRO, EVA FRANCH I. GILABERT, MICHAEL KUBO, BRIAN TABOLT**

Color Separations and Printing: ORO Group Ltd.
Printed in China.

Text printed using offset sheetfed printing process in 5 color on 157gsm premium matt art paper with an off-line gloss acqueous spot varnish applied to all photographs.

ORO editions has made every effort to minimize the overall carbon footprint of this project. As part of this goal, ORO editions, in association with Global ReLeaf, have arranged to plant two trees for each and every tree used in the manufacturing of the paper produced for this book. Global ReLeaf is an international campaign run by American Forests, the nation's oldest nonprofit conservation organization. Global ReLeaf is American Forests' education and action program that helps individuals, organizations, agencies, and corporations improve the local and global environment by planting and caring for trees.

International Distribution:
www.oroeditions.com

CONTENTS

Peter Reyner Banham, Buffalo, 1978
Image courtesy University Archives, State University of New York at Buffalo

Peter Reyner Banham, the renowned architectural historian and cultural critic, taught at the State University of New York at Buffalo between 1976 and 1980. During his tenure at Buffalo, inspired by the daylight factories and the grain silos of the region, he conducted research that led to his seminal book, *A Concrete Atlantis*, theorizing a relationship between American industrial buildings and European Modern Architecture. The Peter Reyner Banham Fellowship program at Buffalo was established in 2000 to celebrate Banham's legacy at Buffalo, and, most importantly, to project new work that is inspired by his foundational body of critical scholarship on material and visual culture. This book documents the research conducted in Buffalo by five Banham Fellows between 2005 and 2010.

INTRODUCTION : MEHRDAD HADIGHI

Peter Reyner Banham, the renowned architectural historian and cultural critic, taught at the State University of New York at Buffalo between 1976 and 1980. During his tenure at Buffalo, inspired by the daylight factories and the grain silos of the region, he conducted research that led to his seminal book, *A CONCRETE ATLANTIS*, theorizing a relationship between American industrial buildings and European Modern Architecture. The Peter Reyner Banham Fellowship program at Buffalo was established in 2000 to celebrate Banham's legacy at Buffalo, and, most importantly, to project new work that is inspired by his foundational body of critical scholarship on material and visual culture. This book documents the research conducted in Buffalo by five Banham Fellowship winners between 2005 and 2010.

Peter Reyner Banham, born in 1922, had a keen interest in engineering and apprenticed in an aircraft company during World War II. Although later he studied history of art and architecture, his love of engineering, specially, of technology for extreme conditions did not leave him. In fact technology and extremes shaped his entire career. Banham began as an architectural historian by writing about iconic buildings, master architects, and historical moments that have shaped our understanding of architecture and history. His first few books did precisely that. With wit, and theoretically astute research, he re-imagined modern architecture in terms of its reception provided by media and through its relationship with technology. Later, he applied the same intense research to an entirely different set of situations: situations that were at the far extremes of the European urban conditions in which he lived and worked. What may, to our eyes today, not seem as radical as it was then. Banham began to examine the everyday landscapes, built and natural, as resources as profound as iconic ancient cathedrals and Corbusian villas.

He looked to America for the everyday landscape: the industrial buildings of Buffalo, the expansive spaces of the deserts of the American Southwest, and Los Angeles, the new urban paradigm. Banham left University College in London, where he taught architecture history, and moved to America in 1976. He charted a trek across the country, with which he coincided teaching engagements at the University at Buffalo, and University of California Santa Cruz. These locations served not only as his home while he was teaching, but more as the site of his new research. Here, he conducted research by personally engaging the everyday landscapes of these locations. This was a different kind of research, one fueled by personal intrigue that required an astute ability to analyze and theorize situations that had not been theorized prior.

His last few books are documents which start by Banham's recognition that there is something absolutely amazing and fascinating in these landscapes. He asks himself why these are interesting places and how and where they fit within the larger context of architectural history. He takes the reader on a journey in search of possible answers. With eyes wide open, critical engagement, and a unique ability to shape language, Banham finds new paradigms of architecture and urbanity, each filled with contradictions. In a 1972 BBC documentary he referenced Los Angeles as making nonsense of all history and said: "I love it with a passion". He started his career at the center of the discipline of architectural history, with its icons and masters, and ended it by looking at the edges, the very distant edges, where he found delight and intrigue in everyday conditions, and produced a set of books, each a self-reflective quest into the barely-recognizable-as-architecture history.

Banham is one of the most astute readers of architectural and urban conditions. In the same breath, he was able to celebrate Rome with its dense pedestrian-friendly urban environment and the beautiful and curvaceous flow of a highway exit ramp in Los Angeles. He was able to celebrate the daylight factories of Buffalo and its industrial heritage while recognizing its decaying industrial infrastructure. What marked his career was his ability to theorize architectural and urban contradictions, and for that he continuously returned to technology and the extreme edges.

Each year for the past ten years we have celebrated Peter Reyner Banham's contributions by appointing a Banham Fellow, who spends time in Buffalo, teaching, researching, and projecting from the work of Banham. The five Banham Fellows presented here, in this book, all, interestingly, selected one of Banham's later projects as their point of departure. *Megastructure* for Solomon, *Scenes in America Deserta and A Concrete Atlantis* for López-Piñeiro; *Los Angeles the Architecture of Four Ecologies* for Kubo; *Banham Loves LA*, the 1972 film for Franch-Gilabert: and his essay "Frank Lloyd Wright's Wilderness Years" for Tabolt. The books (and film) that were personal, self-reflective, and inquisitive in an entirely different way than Banham's earlier projects.

In his analysis of *Megastructure*, in his book of the same title, Banham set out to elucidate the history as well as the analytical boundaries of megastructures. He argues that by the late 60's the scale of the massive, monumental supporting frame of megastructures became unthinkable, and with it the role of the avant-garde architect. What remained was beyond the control of the architect and in the hands of the public. Banham points to this very moment as the moment of demise of the megastructure model: deserted by the avant-garde, it was left to the establishment as a customary method for maximizing profits from urban redevelopment.

This very moment of disjuncture between the avant-garde and the establishment is the point of departure for Solomon's research in Buffalo. Solomon problematizes the relationship between infrastructure and form in the context of the avant-garde. Banham argues that the inability of the megastructure model to reconcile the avant-garde and the establishment is the fundamental cause of its demise as a planning model. Solomon begins his projections at this problematic: how can the avant-garde work within the infrastructure of the establishment? His interest lies in an avant-garde infrastructure, and not in avant-garde form.

López-Piñeiro weaves back and forth between *Scenes in America Deserta* and *A Concrete Atlantis*. Utilizing Banham's proposition that the desert is the paradigmatic modern space, defined by its minimal, sparse infinity, he maps, repetitively, the space of that infinity onto the interior of a prototypical daylight factory, the paradigmatic industrial building typology that Banham cited as the link to European modern architecture.

Kubo takes Banham's 1971 book, *Los Angeles the Architecture of Four Ecologies* as his inspiration. Kubo, in his examination of the relationship between architectural publishing and practice, also seeks to highlight why Banham, with the publication of this book, a year ahead of Venturi and Scott-Brown's *Learning from Las Vegas*, and his involvement with the Independent Group and their 1956 "This is tomorrow" exhibition-considered as the birth-venue of the pop movement-has not had as much readership as Venturi and Scott-Brown, and finally, why his is not the name associated with the pop movement in architecture. This question is examined in a thorough survey and analysis of the relationships between iconic books, their authors, and the history of architecture as we have come to know it.

Franch-Gilabert frames a series of points that Banham raises in the BBC documentary on LA, *Banham Loves LA*, as trajectories to be pursued by today's architects. She poses each point as a way of introducing "doubt" in the foundation of any search for utopia.

Tabolt, fascinated by Banham's interest in the relationship of architecture and urbanism, more specifically the contradictions embedded in the application of architectural form to urbanism, and architectural ideas to urban form, deciphers from Banham's LA projects a kind of "drifting" as a modality of exploring and experiencing a city. He then applies the "drift" as a methodology for design and for a way of negotiating the nuances between the problematic of repetition, embedded in both democracy and industrialization.

Banham was able to put his finger on the extremes of contradictions. In Los Angeles, for example, he notes the freedom and the pleasure of speeding along a sweeping highway exit ramp on one extreme, and the gated communities of BelAire where free movement is absolutely ceased, on the other. With the conception of the Banham Fellowship program at Buffalo our hope has been to highlight the diversity of Banham's research by providing an environment that encourages each Fellow to project new itineraries for research and trajectories for scholarship and design, starting from and fueled by the work of Peter Reyner Banham.

Peter Reyner Banham was born on March 2, 1922 in Norwich, England. He had always been interested in engineering and apprenticed in an aircraft company during World War II, but later shifted his interest to the study of the history of art and architecture. He received his doctorate in 1958 from the Courtauld Institute of Art in London, where he studied with Anthony Blunt, Siegfried Giedion and Nikolaus Pevsner. Beginning in 1952 he served on the editorial staff of the Architectural Review magazine, where he remained till 1964, when he started teaching at the University College in London. He taught there till 1976, when he moved to the United States to join the faculty at Buffalo. In 1980, he became professor of art history at the University of California at Santa Cruz, where he remained till 1988, when he was named the Sheldon H. Solow Professor of the History of Architecture at the Institute of Fine Arts at NYU. He was unable to take on this last engagement due to illness, and died in London on March 19, 1988 at the age of 66. His last book, *A Concrete Atlantis,* which he researched and prepared while in Buffalo, appeared in 1989, after his death.

PETER REYNER BANHAM BOOKS:

Theory and Design in the First Machine Age. Praeger. 1960.

Theory and Design in the First Machine Age: Second Edition. Praeger. 1967.

Guide to Modern Architecture. Architectural Press. 1962.

The New Brutalism. Architectural Press. 1966.

Architecture of the Well-tempered Environment. Architectural Press. 1969.

Architecture of the Well-tempered Environment: Second, Revised Edition. Architectural Press. 1984.

Los Angeles The Architecture Of Four Ecologies. Harper and Row. 1971.

Megastructure. Thames and Hudson Ltd. 1976. Scenes in America Deserta. Thames and Hudson. 1982.

A Concrete Atlantis: US Industrial Building and European Modern Architecture. MIT Press. 1989.

Megastructure in Academe
152
153
152, 153 Fitzrovia traffic reorganization proposals, London (Buchanan research team members Haxworth, Woodward, Richardson, 1962). The classic half-mile-square site of a typical sixties urban renewal scheme, completely decked over with a new pedestrian podium (black in 152) twenty feet above ground level, the road system organized on an ideal hexagonal grid traversed by multi-lane super-highways at a far closer spacing than had been proposed for even the most 'motor-mad' American cities, and topped with development as solid as in Gruen's Fort Worth (see 40). Though the effect on architectural and planning professionals was galvanic, not even Kenneth Browne's skilful perspectives (153) could make the result look attractive to the man in the street.
strength of their
management for
was extreme, its
direct influence,
the British Civil
proper solution for
In this
world's other
socially and even
and official planning
of footing in the
remarkably
planted within the
cities were under
After 1963
architecture and the
particular, an
under the
emphasis on the
seventy thousand
urban structure
country
that
the intentions
all levels; make an
and utopianisms of
mere functionalism;
architectural languages,
146

The most striking question left behind by this feverish activity must always be: from whence came the self-confidence, the sheer nerve, to propose works of such urban complexity and vast scale...

Peter Reyner Banham, *Megastructure: Urban Futures of the Recent Past* (London: Thames and Hudson, 1976), 10.

LOOKING FOR MEGASTRUCTURE: A PARTIAL ARCHAEOLOGY OF THE PRESENT

JONATHAN D. SOLOMON

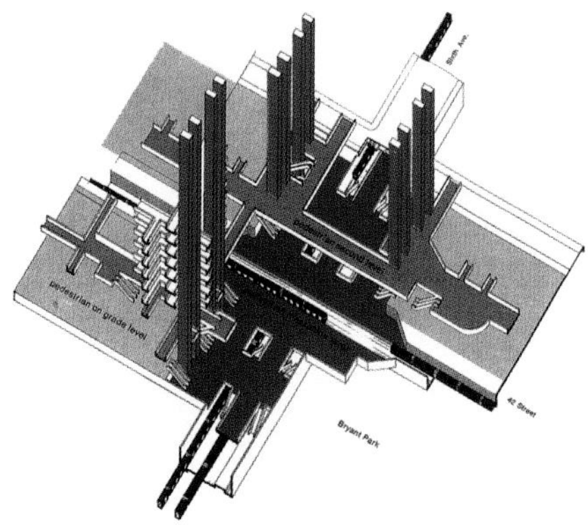

In 1976, architectural historian Peter Reyner Banham published the book *Megastructure: Urban Futures of the Recent Past*. A monograph on a "self-canceling concept," *Megastructure* catalogs the rise and demise of a heroic but deeply faulted period of architecture culture. Banham locates the failure of the megastructure as a concept first in the critique of modernist planning and of "comprehensible design" in all fields that developed in the postwar period and second in the overabundance of faith in "self-determining" systems to replace them. In the first case, the megastructure proved too firmly tethered to the sinking ships of centralized planning: socialist governments, urban redevelopment projects, state expositions, and top-down university expansions. In the second case, where these faults were perceived, "the logical solution to the problem was to leave so much liberty for the self-housing and self determining intentions of the inhabitants that they had liberty also to destroy the megastructure itself."[1]

For Banham, *Megastructure* the book was a platform for broader critique of the proclivities and tendencies of architects. Megastructure the concept, for all its difficulties, was clearly enthralling to him, bringing together as it did a number of his interests—technology, environment and culture—in totalizing schemes for the unification of architecture and the city. It was the fact that architects could fall so blindly for it that made the movement so perfect for Banham's tragicomedy. *Megastructure*, and the "terminal crisis" of modernism it coincided with, turned the megastructure into a cliché in architecture schools; but the book, when seen as the final installment of a trilogy including *Los Angeles: The Architecture of Four Ecologies* and *Architecture of the Well-Tempered Environment*, opens more doors than it closes.

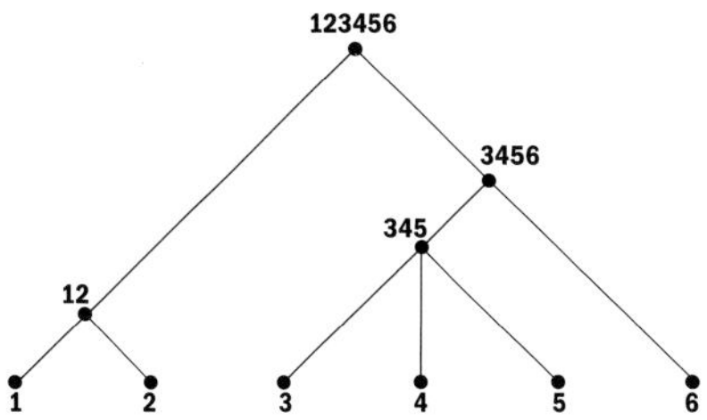

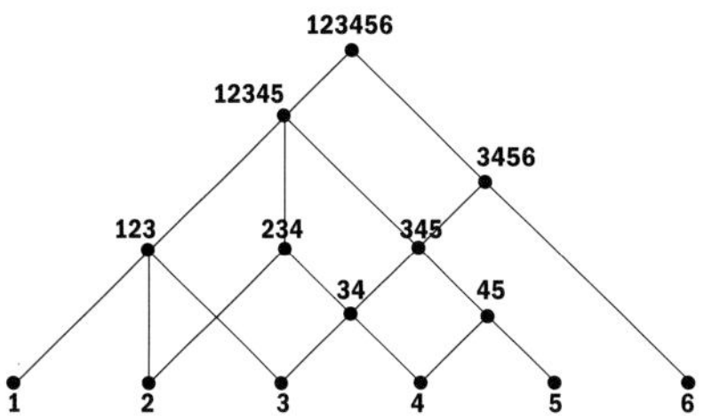

Cosympathisers with Banham and the optimism of his "Futures of the Recent Past" will appreciate that a partial archaeology of the present reveals the persistence of megastructure at surprising scale and ambition—if perhaps in new terms. Looking for megastructure today, we find access networks—continuous but heterogeneous climate-controlled interiors, publicly accessible but privately owned and with close relationships to transit and shopping programs, access networks are atmospheric megastructures.

How did access networks arise where megastructure failed? Banham credits megastructure's original appeal with its ability to reconcile the designed and the spontaneous, the large and the small, the permanent and the transient; and he locates its downfall in its inability to reconcile the avant-garde and the establishment. By the 1970s "Megastructure," Banham writes, "deserted by the avant garde, was left to the despised establishment as a conventional method for maximizing the returns of urban development."[2] This is precisely where the history of access networks begins, where public utility meets private profit, where regional design meets local use, where emergent organization necessary for market forces to function meets the regulatory structure necessary to secure broad public appeal.

Christopher Alexander's 1965 "The City is not a Tree," and the "Access Tree," a concept introduced in the Regional Plan Association's 1969 publication *Urban Design Manhattan*, exemplify the era's struggle to reconcile the top-down and bottom-up planning principles that Banham identifies with the avante-garde and establishment, respectively. While megastructure's

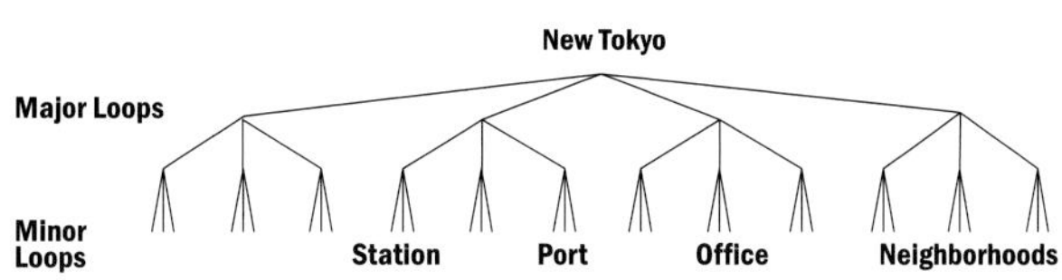

ACCESS TREE, 1969

The Access Tree, from the Regional Plan Association's 1969 *Urban Design Manhattan*. Image courtesy of the Regional Plan Association.

TREE AND SEMILATTICE, 1965

Christopher Alexander's comparative diagrams of a Semilattice (top) and a Tree (middle), and diagram of Tange's Tokyo Bay project as a Tree hierarchy (below).

eventual collapse as a viable political or intellectual movement in architecture, according to Banham, came about as a result of establishment organization and avant-garde expression, today's access networks exhibit avant-garde organization and establishment expression. Because access networks rely not on the image of connections, but rather on thresholds between discrete atmospheres and activities, they succeed by operating like megastructure without looking like it. These vast urban semilattices, hot in winter and cool in summer, are invisible but far from irrelevant.

Megastructure offered architects an alternative vision for structuring the city of the future, a vision that, in Banham's assessment, was terminally compelling. Access networks succeed in creating such new structures through tangible but invisible atmospheres; ecologies tempered by assemblies of independent climate control systems, creating distinctions between the hot and the cold, the humid and the dry, the lit and the dark. Access networks come about neither through centralized planning nor unfettered liberty, but rather as a result of market systems that limit self-organizing forces with robust regulatory structures. Operating in the same way, they reconcile the formal flows of people with the informal flows of information and capital that drive the development of the contemporary city. Access networks provide the continuity of space on which both flows rely: air-conditioned connections from the train to the museum, a bright passage at night from the parking lot to the office, and a dry walk between shopping malls in the rain. Banham, it is safe to suggest, would have found them terribly interesting.

NOTES

1 Peter Reyner Banham, *Megastructure: Urban Futures of the Recent Past (London: Thames and Hudson, 1976), 218.*

2 Banham, *Megastructure,* 10.

ACCESS NETWORKS: HOUSTON, SHANGHAI, PARIS

The Houston tunnel system is an Access Network. Over six miles of air conditioned tunnels connect ninety-five city blocks. People's Park is an Access Network. Above ground a large open space filled with outsized public buildings erected atop the former cricket grounds of the British Concession serves a representational role, while below, pedestrian passages and shopping corridors link three Metro stations to surrounding malls and Nanjing Road. A similar situation occurs at the Louvre Palace in Paris, where an underground mall joins the museum entrance directly to an adjacent, existing Metro station. The Louvre is an Access Network. (Above) Houston Tunnel System. (Middle) People's Park, Shanghai. (Below) The Lourve Paris. Drawings p. 17-21 by the author.

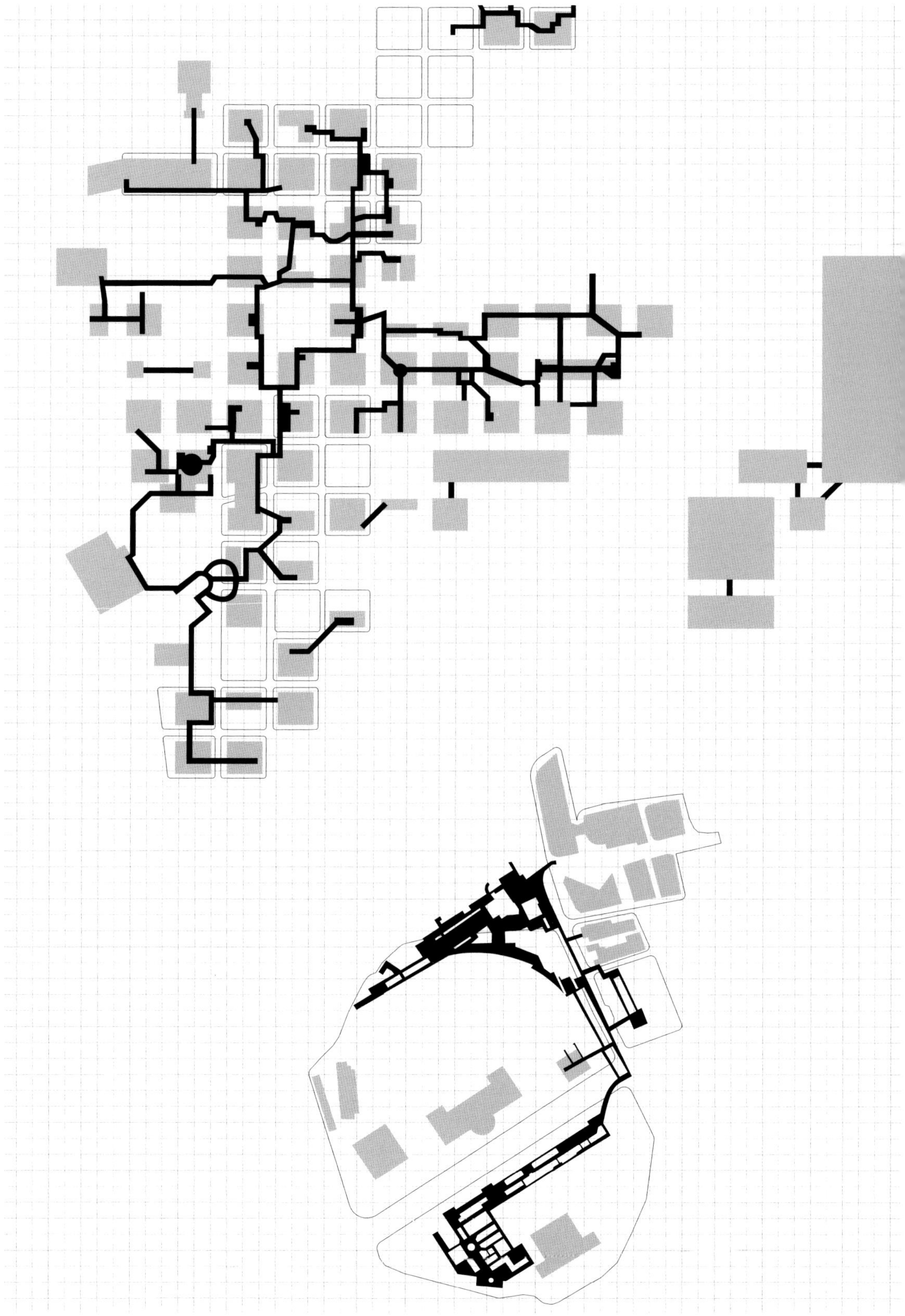

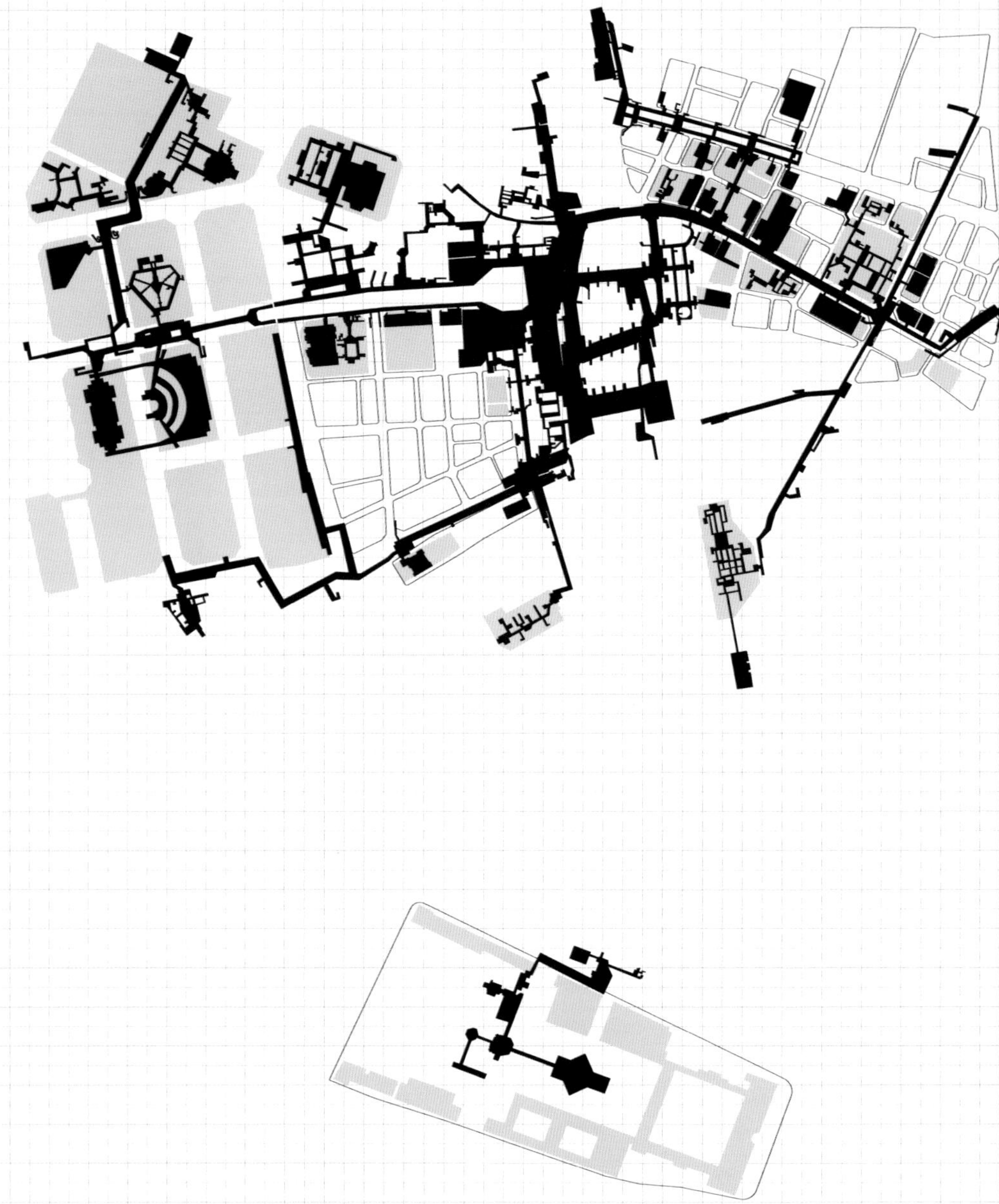

ACCESS NETWORK: TOKYO

Shinjuku is an Access Network. Banham identifies an early Megastructure in Maki and Otaka's 1962 project for the new development of Shinjuku, an example of a large scale government-financed infrastructure project which would serve as a literal new ground for private development.

The underground pedestrian networsk that binds Shinjuku today emerged through a different process: As private developers saw the benefit in drawing foot traffic through connections to the public network, they financed its extension. (Above) Shinjuku Station, Tokyo.

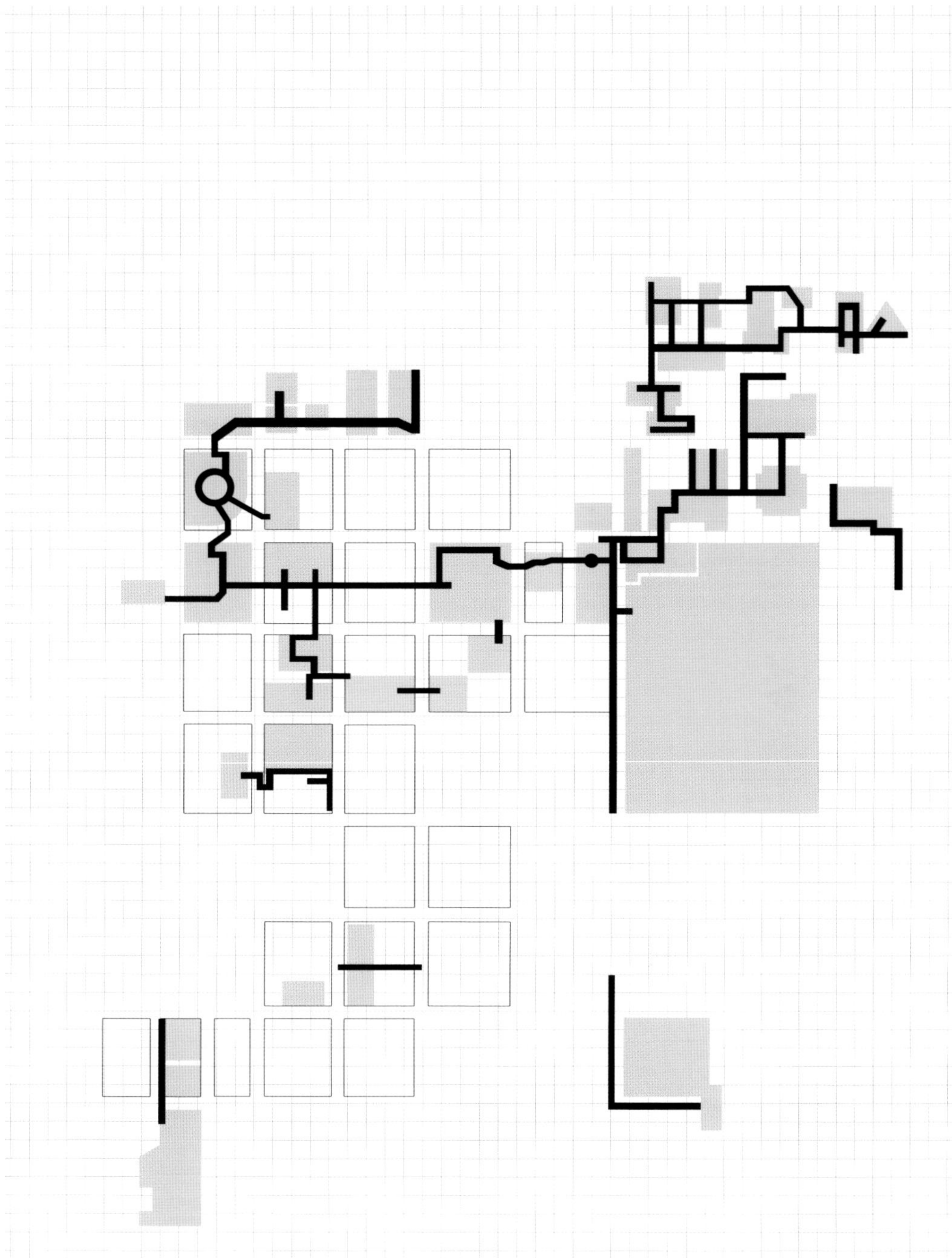

ACCESS NETWORK: CHICAGO

Dating back to 1939, the Chicago Pedway links over 40 downtown blocks via tunnels, ground level arcades, and skyways. (Above) The Chicago Pedway.

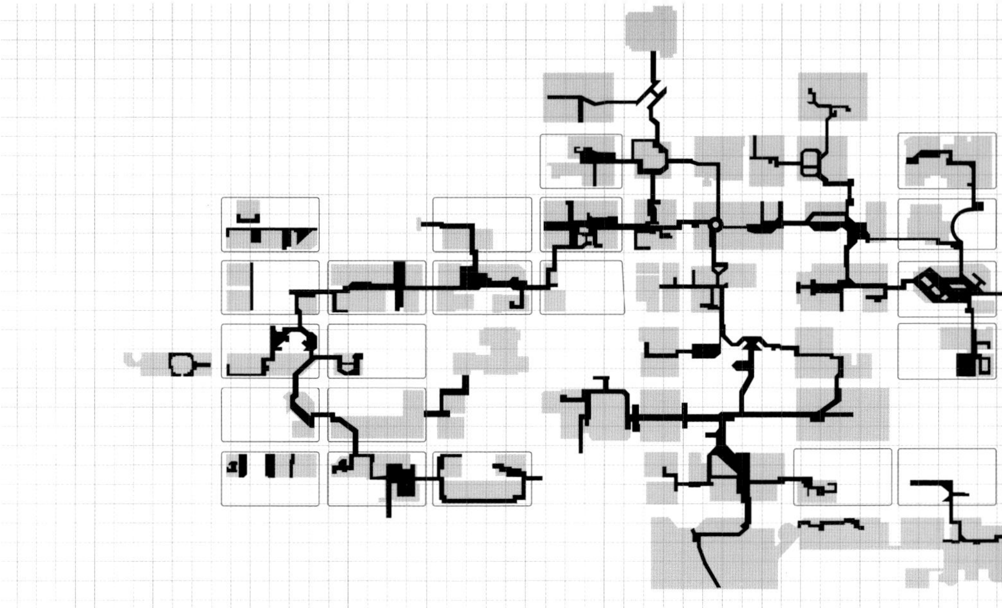

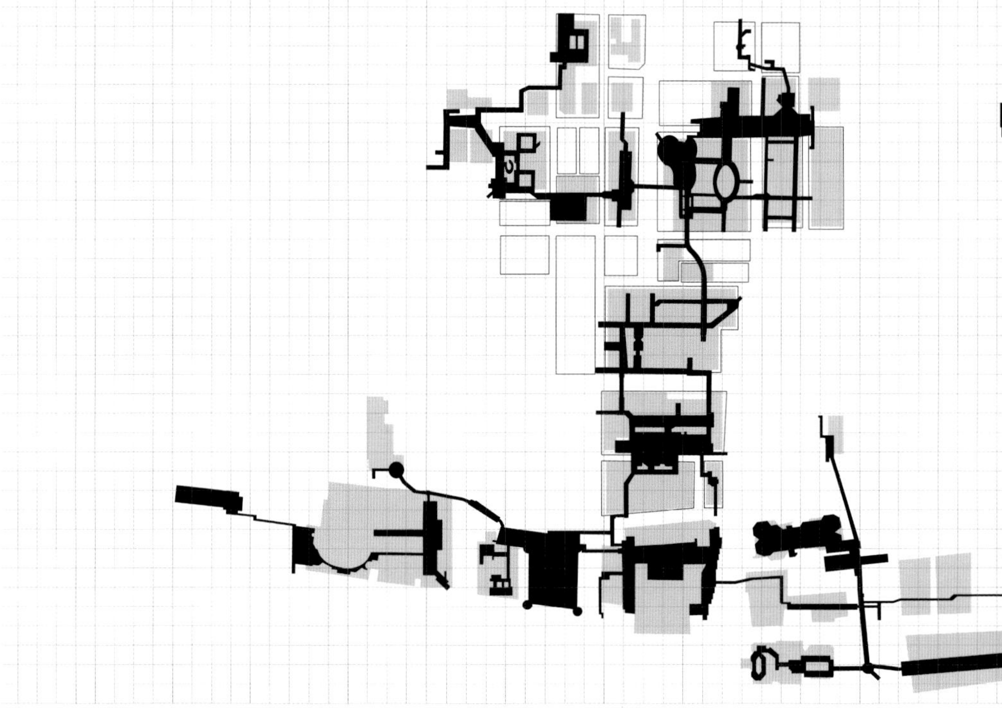

ACCESS NETWORKS: CALGARY, MONTREAL...

Banham devotes an entire chapter of Megastructure to "Megacity Montreal," with a focus on the 1967 Expo and on the then emerging underground city of the downtown, which he credits to ad-hoc public-private opportunism of Vincent Ponte and William Zeckendorf, Place Ville Marie, and Affleck's Place Bonaventure. Subsequently, Montreal (today's RESO) and a host of North American cities with diverse climates have developed armatures at extraordinary scale and complexity, creaing entire cities over or under the ground plane. (Above) Calgary's +15 Skyways. (Below) Montreal's RESO tunnel system.

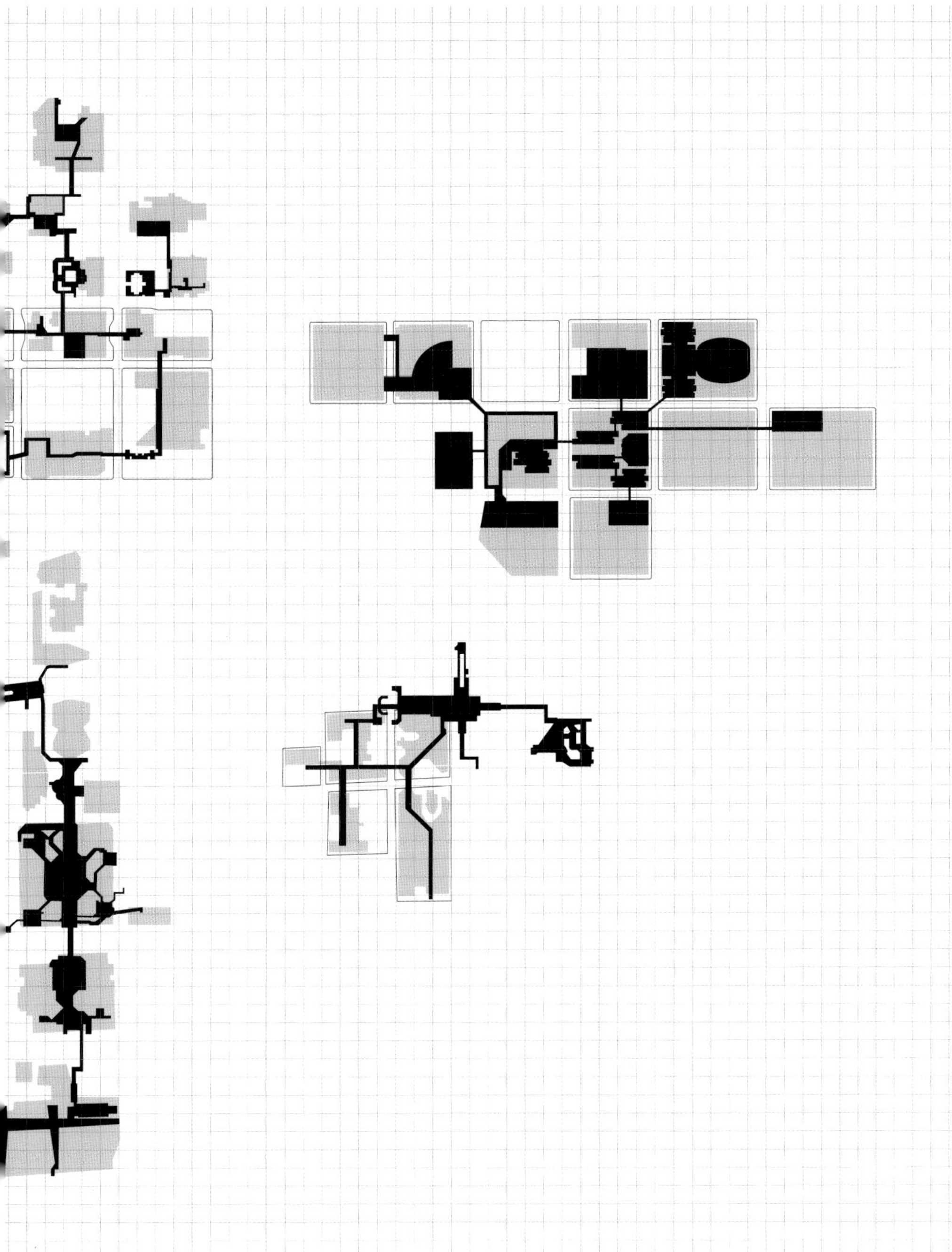

ACCESS NETWORK: ATLANTA

Peachtree Center is an Access Network. Begining in 1961, John Portman & Associates developed individual parcels in Downtown Atlanta and linked them with a three-dimensional network of interior public passages. The link to public transit came later, with the opening of the Peachtree Center MARTA station in 1982. (Above) Peachtree Center, Atlanta.

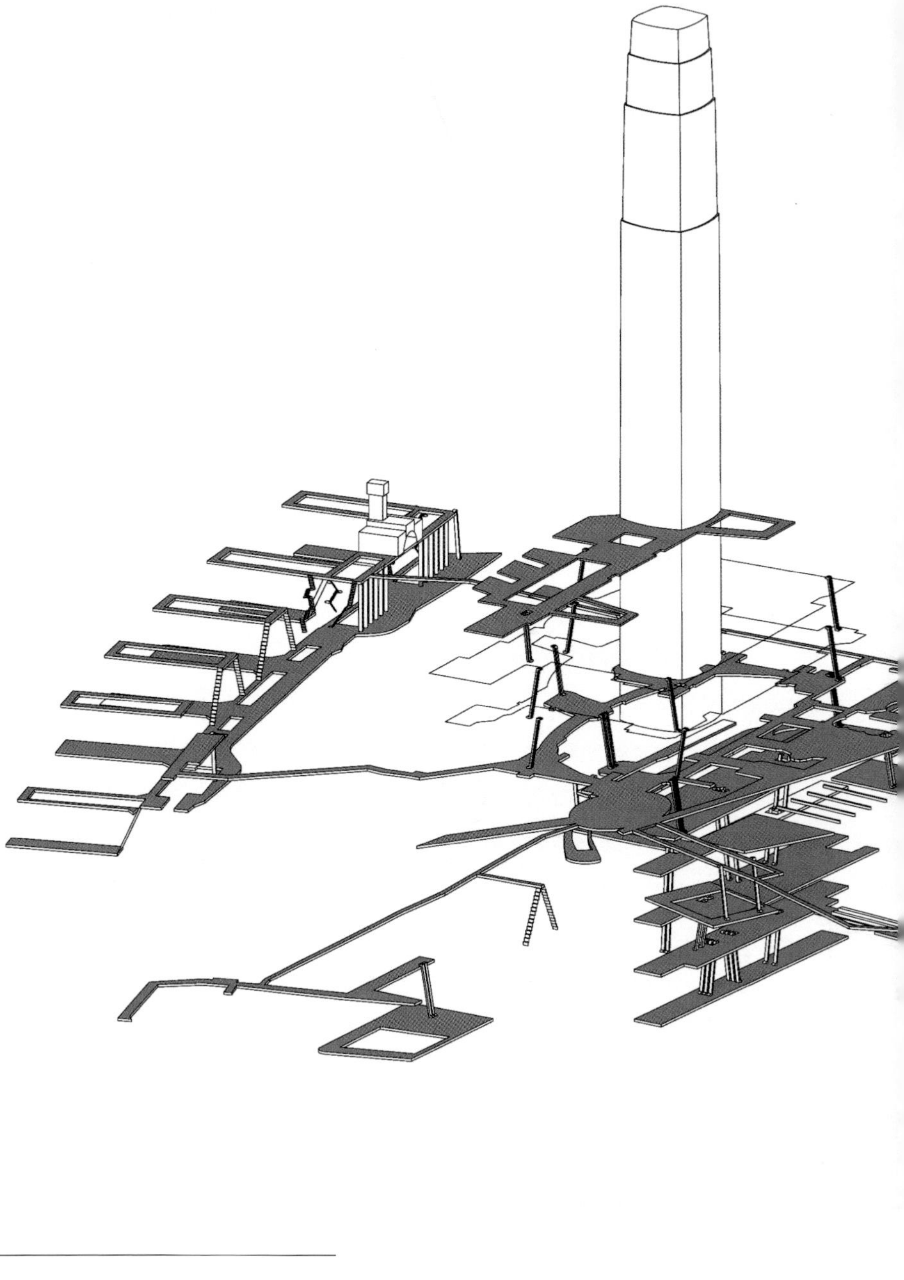

ACCESS NETWORK: HONG KONG

Interconnected shopping malls in Hong Kong are Access Networks. Built piecemeal, owned by different public and private stakeholders, and adjacent to different programs and uses, Access Networks form a continuous pedestrian armature stretching over several miles along the north shore of Hong Kong Island. Drawing by Jonathan D Solomon and Clara Wong.

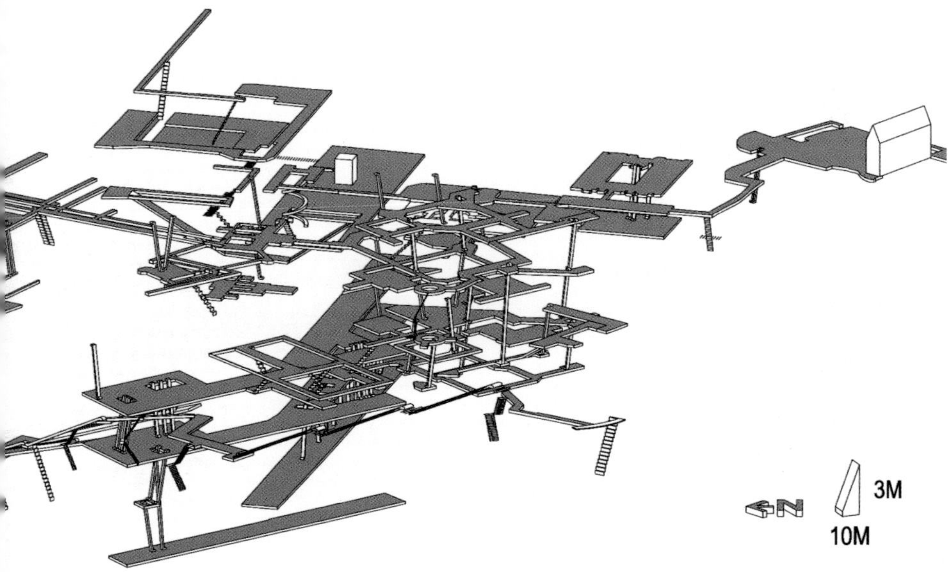
3M
10M

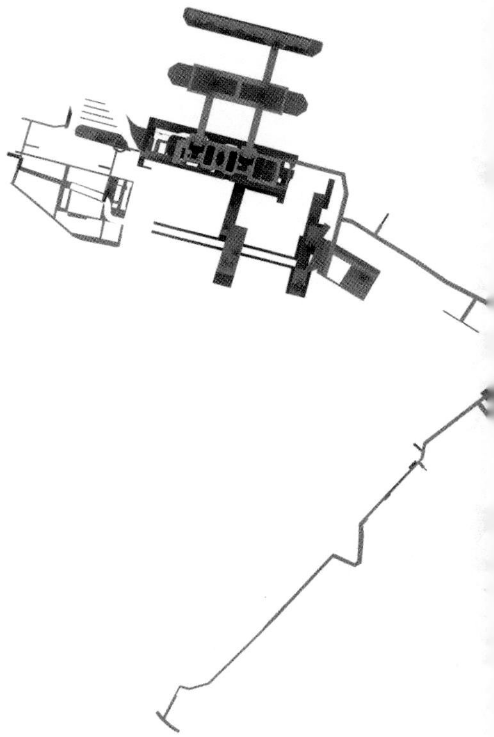

ACCESS NETWORK: HONG KONG

The Access Network in Hong Kong is unique in its degree of three-dimensional integration and its variety of climates. Drawing by Adam Frampton, Jonathan D Solomon and Clara Wong.

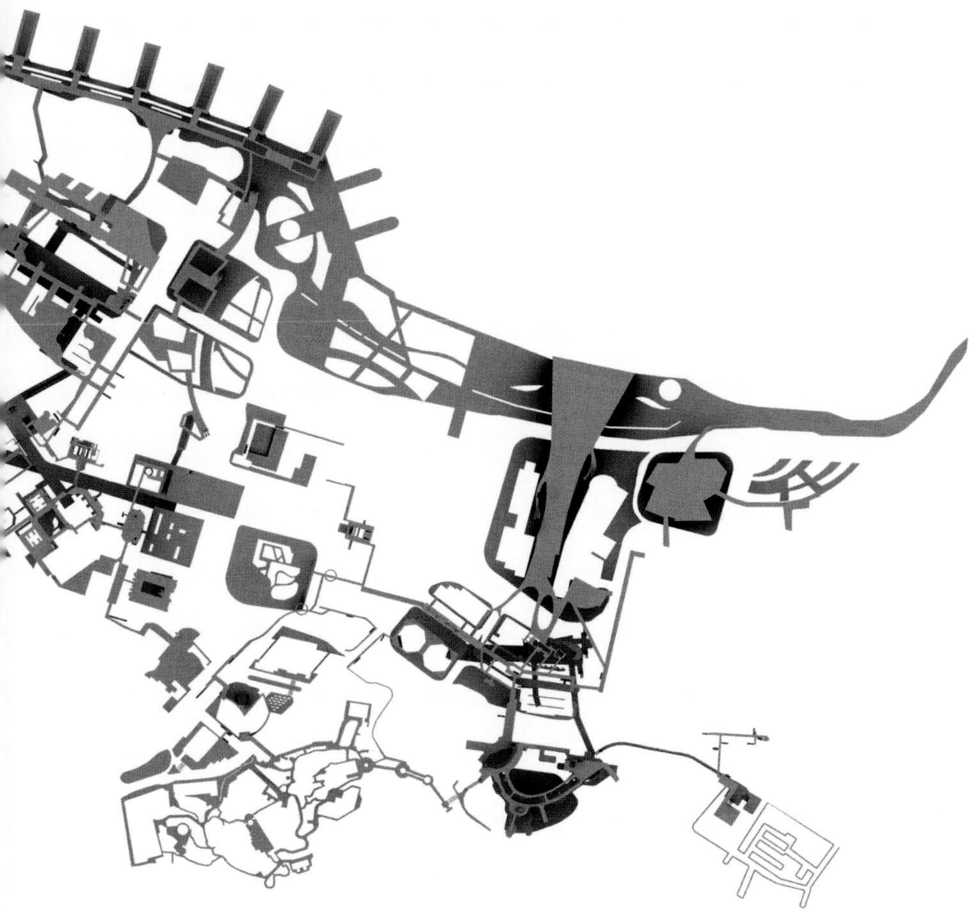

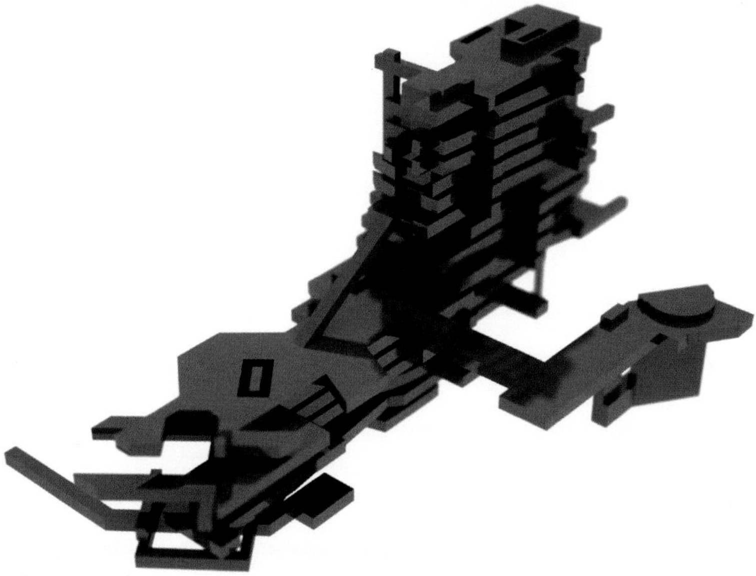

SELECTIONS FROM ACCESS STORY, 2009

Void spaces of public passage networks in two Hong Kong shopping malls rendered as positive casts demonstrate the figural qualities of interior space in the city. Drawings by Jonathan D Solomon and Clara Wong.

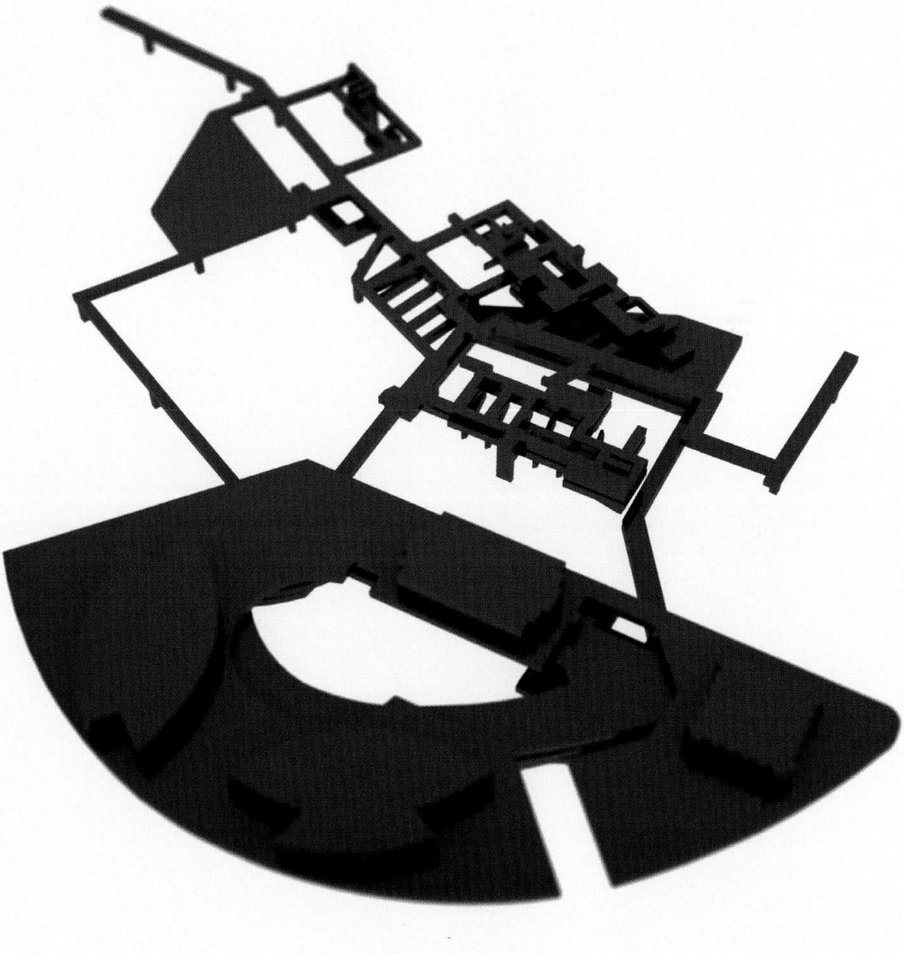

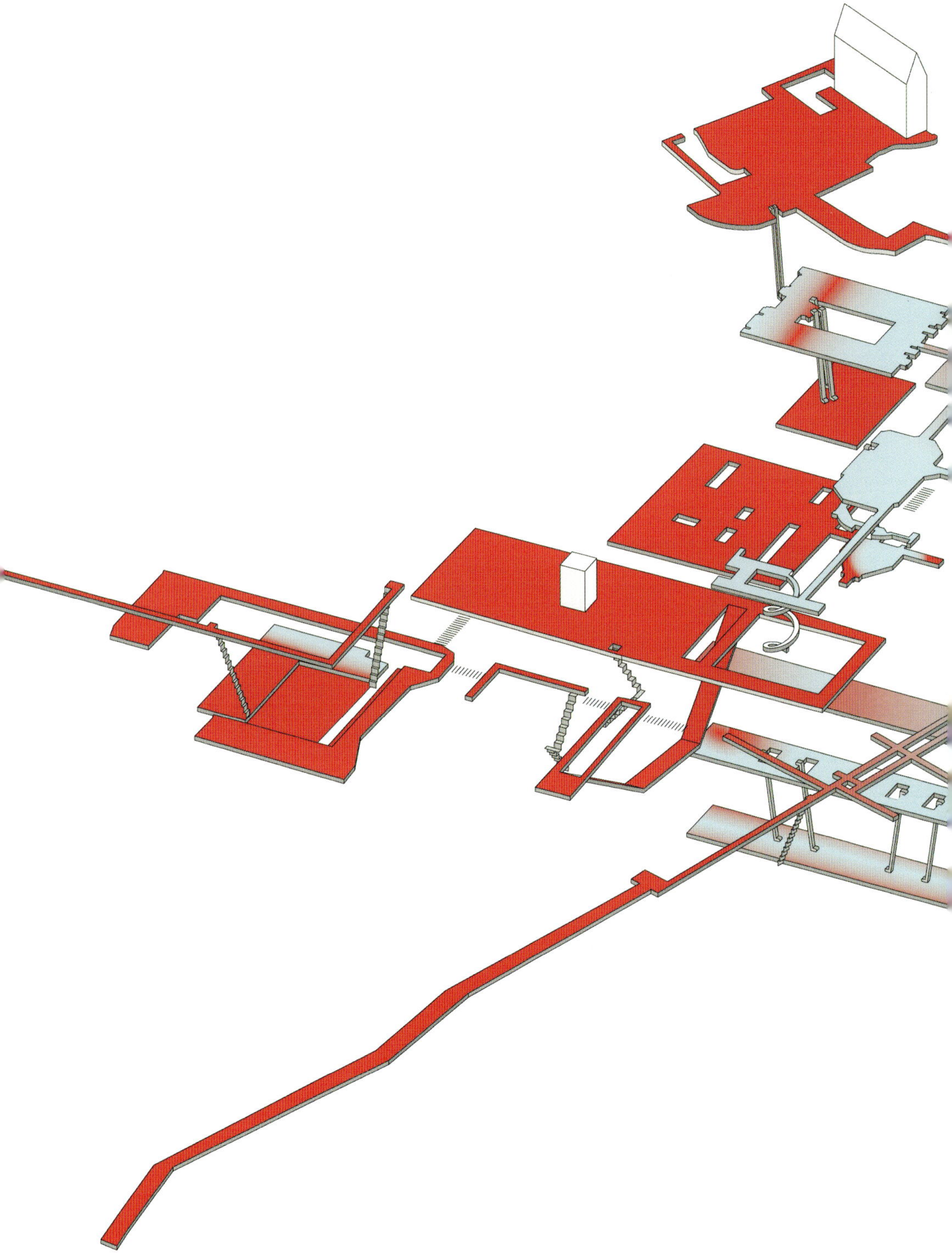

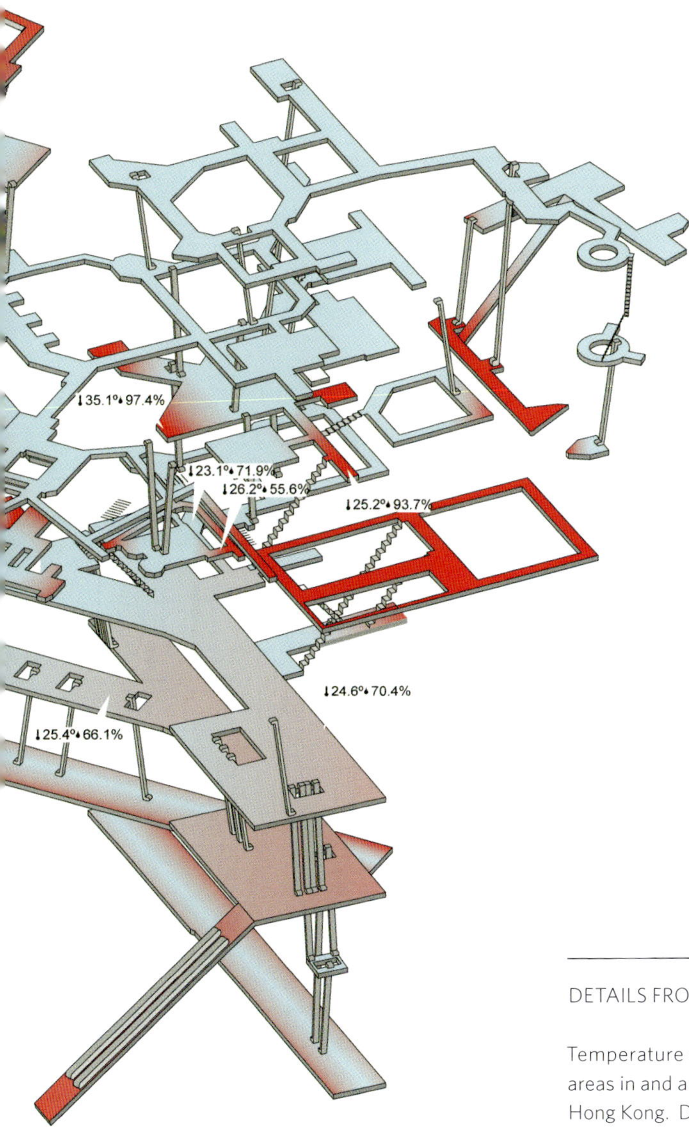

DETAILS FROM THERMALLMETER, 2010

Temperature differentials in pedestrian passage areas in and around the Landmark Mall, Central, Hong Kong. Drawing by Adam Frampton, Jonathan D Solomon and Clara Wong. Research Support by Hong Kong Clean Air Network and Airtek.

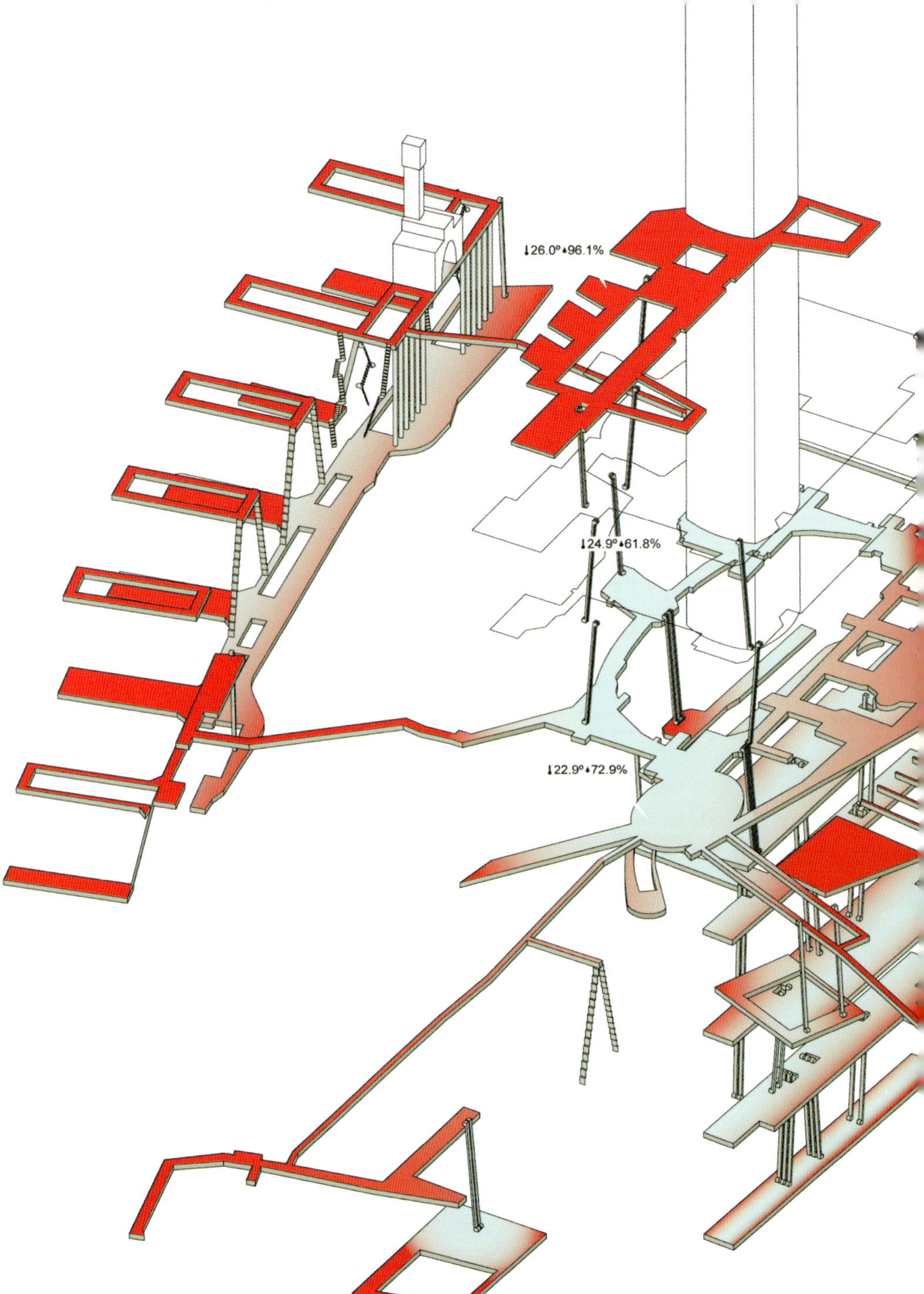
↓26.0°•96.1%
↓24.9°•61.8%
↓22.9°•72.9%

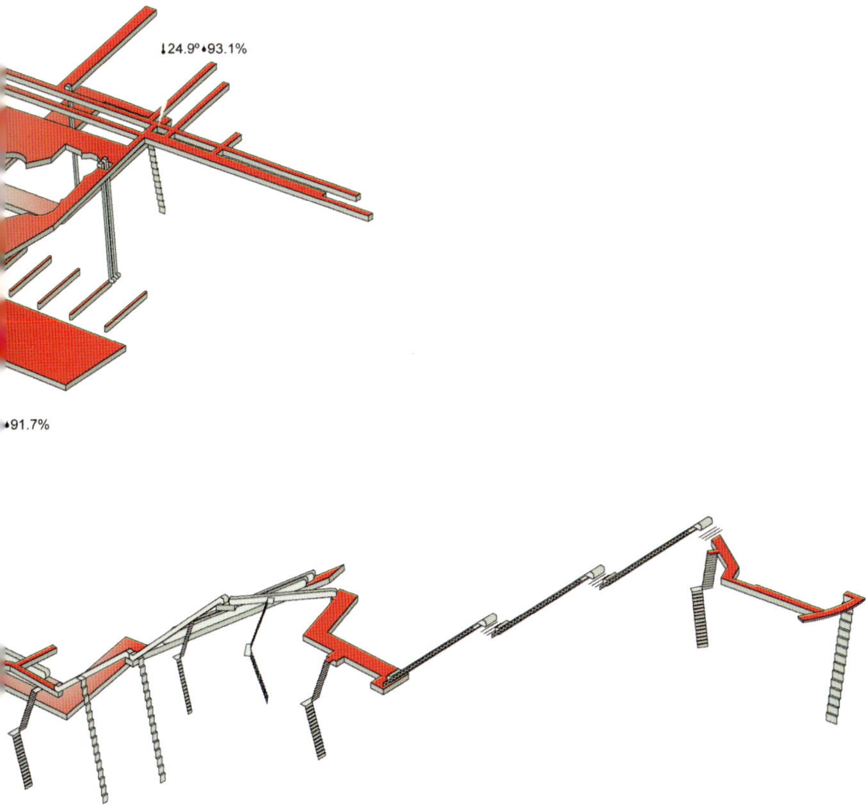

DETAILS FROM THERMALLMETER, 2010

Temperature differentials in pedestrian passage areas in and around the Landmark Mall, Central, Hong Kong. Drawing by Adam Frampton, Jonathan D Solomon and Clara Wong. Research Support by Hong Kong Clean Air Network and Airtek.

Cleaned and abandoned, with vast windows and endless rows of regular repetitive columns, these clean well-lighted spaces have an uncanny and deeply reassuring calm. The noise and bustle of production, the bulging accumulations of racked products, have long departed. All that remain are rational frameworks for human activities—awaiting their orders. But even in what remains of Ford's "Old Shop" at Highland Park, the only American site that has anything like the historical importance and cultural consequences of Lingotto, they are just neutral containers for which alternative uses, if any, will be found by the normal mechanisms of the market economy.

Peter Reyner Banham, "Fiat: The Phantom of Order" in *A Critic Writes,* Mary Banham, ed., (Berkeley and Los Angeles: University of California Press, 1996), 260.

SCENES IN A CONCRETE DESERTA

SERGIO LOPEZ-PIÑEIRO

In his last two books, *Scenes in America Deserta* (1982) and *A Concrete Atlantis* (1986), Peter Reyner Banham presented two complementary arguments regarding the agreements and disagreements between Modern Architecture (and its development as the International Style) and two American idiosyncratic spaces: the desert and the daylight factory. Although it seems that Banham had been thinking about the desert since 1970,[1] it was surely not a coincidence that both titles were finally written and published after he had moved to the United States in 1976.

A Concrete Atlantis pointed out the influence of the typical American daylight factory upon the International Style. Coincidentally, Bethune Hall—formerly Buffalo Meter Company (1915)—the building where Banham first taught after arriving in the United States, exemplifies, in the book, this unique American space. The influence noted by Banham is primarily spatial—not so much an issue of style—and demonstrates that European Modern spatiality is grounded on American spaces of production.

REYNER BANHAM AND THE DESERT

(Previous page) Peter Reyner Banham biking through Silurian Lake in California. Photo: Tim Street-Porter.

In *Scenes in America Deserta*, his most personal and least understood book, Banham wonders why the immeasurable space offered by the desert, which seems to be so well aligned with Modernity's immense spatial nature, does not appeal as comfortably to the "Modern Man" (surely a European?): "The sense of vast immensity is not phony; the desert measurably offers immeasurable space. It is therefore an environment in which "Modern Man" ought to feel at home—his modern painting, as in the works of Mondrian, implies a space that extends beyond the confines of the canvas; his modern architecture, as in the works of Mies van

der Rohe, is a rectangular partition of a regular but infinite space; its ideal inhabitants, the sculptures of Giacometti stalking metaphysically through that space as far as it infinitely extends. And modern man's last frontier of exploration, in case you'd forgotten, is space itself—which is how we came to stumbling about lunar landscapes that are uncomfortably like the deserts of the earth. Yet quite a few modern men are far from comfortable in this limitless immensity; and as one who enjoys it to the point of exultation, I have to wonder whether the inability to do so is cultural or temperamental."[2]

Factories always provide a very powerful spatial experience since their extensive space is bizarrely fulfilling. In most situations this is achieved by the appearance of an interior horizon line produced by the protective extra coat of paint located in the lower half of the columns and reaching up to a person's eye-level. This accidental datum, unique to this type of building, when it is completely empty, provides a very powerful psychological effect making the visitor feel as if in an interior desert.

THE AMERICAN DAYLIGHT FACTORY

The images shown here are three of the many factories designed by Albert Kahn's office, whose work helped define the typical American daylight factory. (Top left) Burroughs Adding Machine Company, Plymouth, Michigan. (Bottom left) Ford Motor Company, Highland Park, Michigan. (Top right) Continental Motors Company, Detroit, Michigan. Photos: Albert Kahn Associates.

"*Scenes in a Concrete Deserta*" explores the mismatching encounters described by Reyner Banham (America vs. Europe, spaces of production vs. spaces of inhabitation, comfort vs.

discomfort in the occupation of immeasurable spaces) through the manipulation of this interior horizon line common to both the desert and the daylight factory. Through the transformation of this single datum into a series of homogeneously distributed virtual volumes, the singular space defined by the horizon line becomes a field of spatial intensities. This transformation, which occurs without altering the space's immeasurable continuity, constitutes a step in my ongoing exploration in defining space as a field of continuous distribution rather than as a materialized singularity.

With few exceptions, architectural works address singular conditions. Whether it is the accumulation of knowledge (library), the place where justice is served (court house), the transport hub (infrastructural node), the commemoration of a specific event (monument), the construction of a commercial brand (iconic building), or the house of God (temple), singularities have almost invariably dominated architects' work. In fact, architecture can be defined as a discipline primarily invested in the materialization of singularities. My work challenges this assumption by proposing blank spaces liberated from externally imposed roles, meanings, or functions. Without its singular nature, architecture is transformed into a framework or a platform for free life. The blank spaces I envision exhibit a democratic and empty homogeneity, enabling all sorts of predicted but also unexpected possibilities.

NOTES

1 According to the "*Reyner Banham Papers* (1930-1990)" archived at The Getty Research Institute. Inventory is accessible online:
http://archives2.getty.edu:8082/xtfview?docId=ead/910009/910009.xml;query=Reyner%20Banham%20;brand=default (accessed June 19, 2011).

2 Peter Reyner Banham, *Scenes in America Deserta* (Salt Lake City: Gibbs M. Smith, 1982), 61-2.

FROM A SINGLE HORIZON TO A SERIES OF VOLUMES

The horizontal datum becomes a homogeneously distributed series of volumes.

All drawings and images of models by the author.

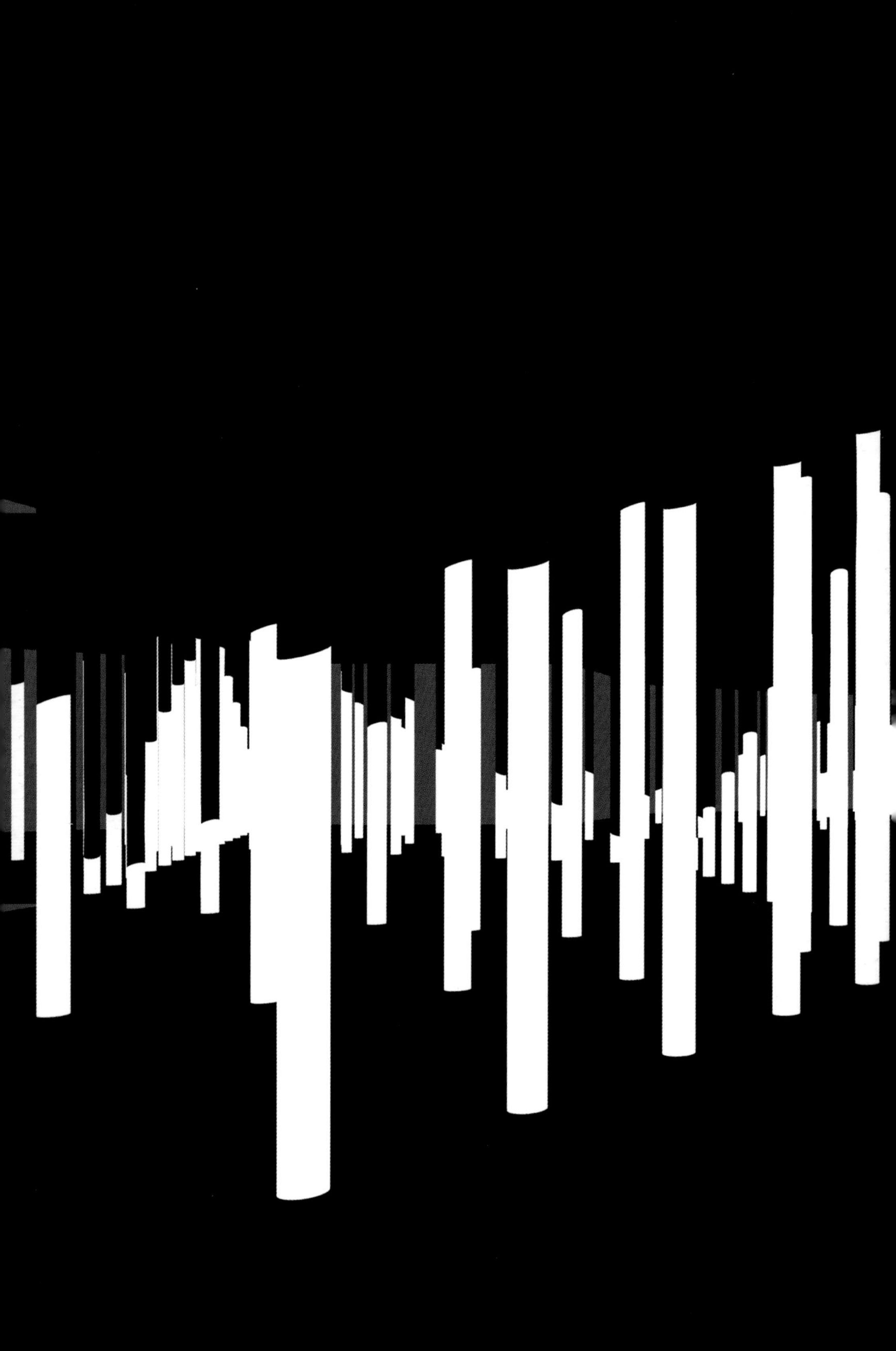

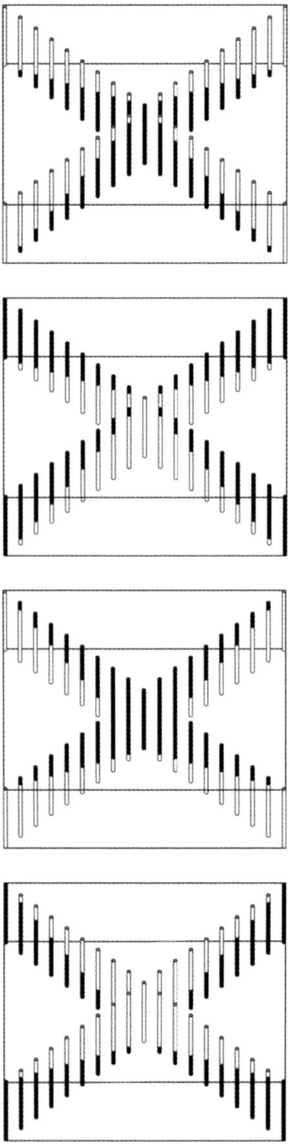

HYPOSTYLED DESERT

(Previous Page) Concrete Deserta produced through the grouping of four octogonal volumes.

ZONES OF INTENSITY

Four variations on the transformation of a homogeneous grid into a zone of spatial intensity.

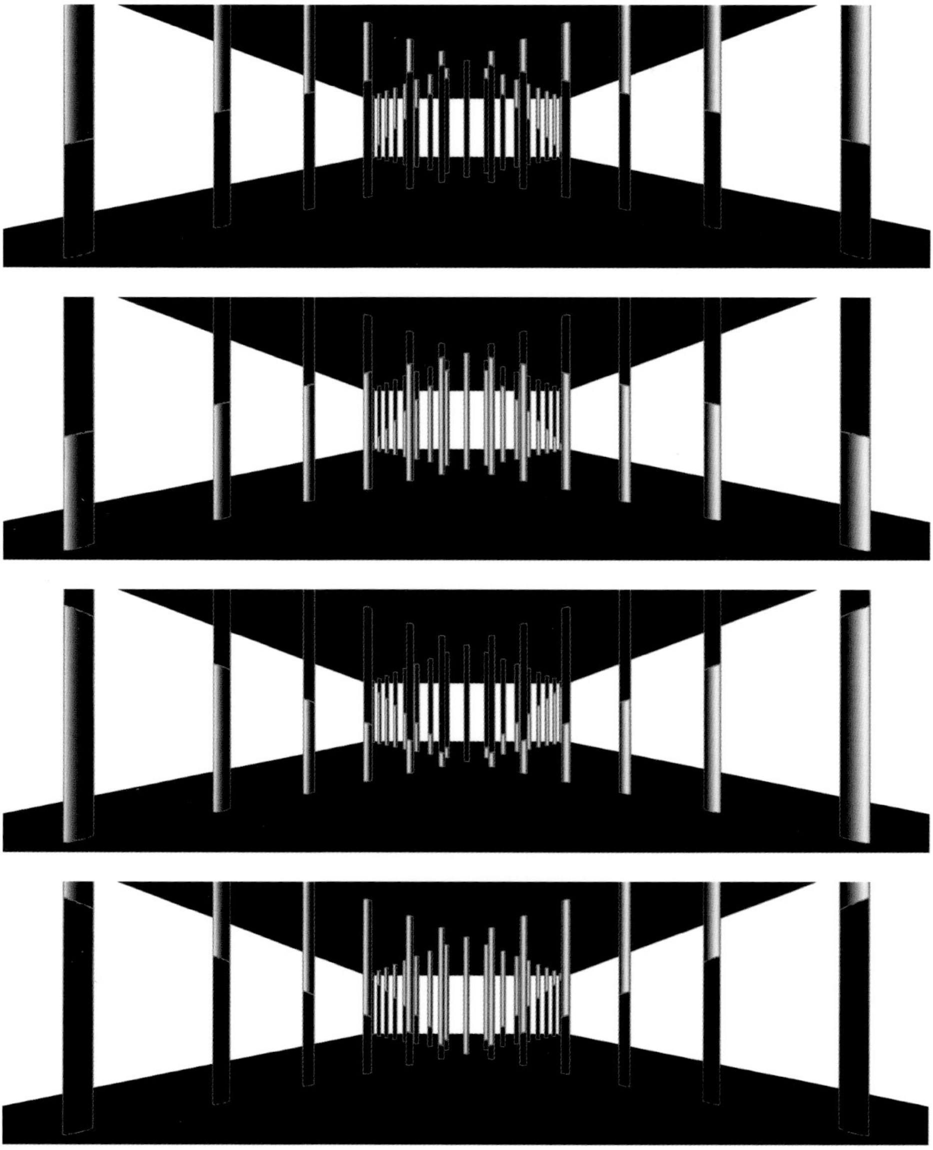

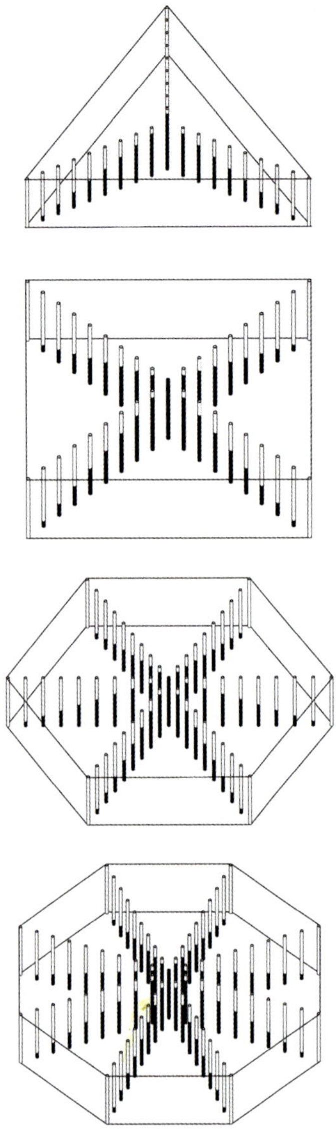

ZONES OF INTENSITY

Unlike grids, zones of intensity are dependent on the limits of the space they influence and organize.

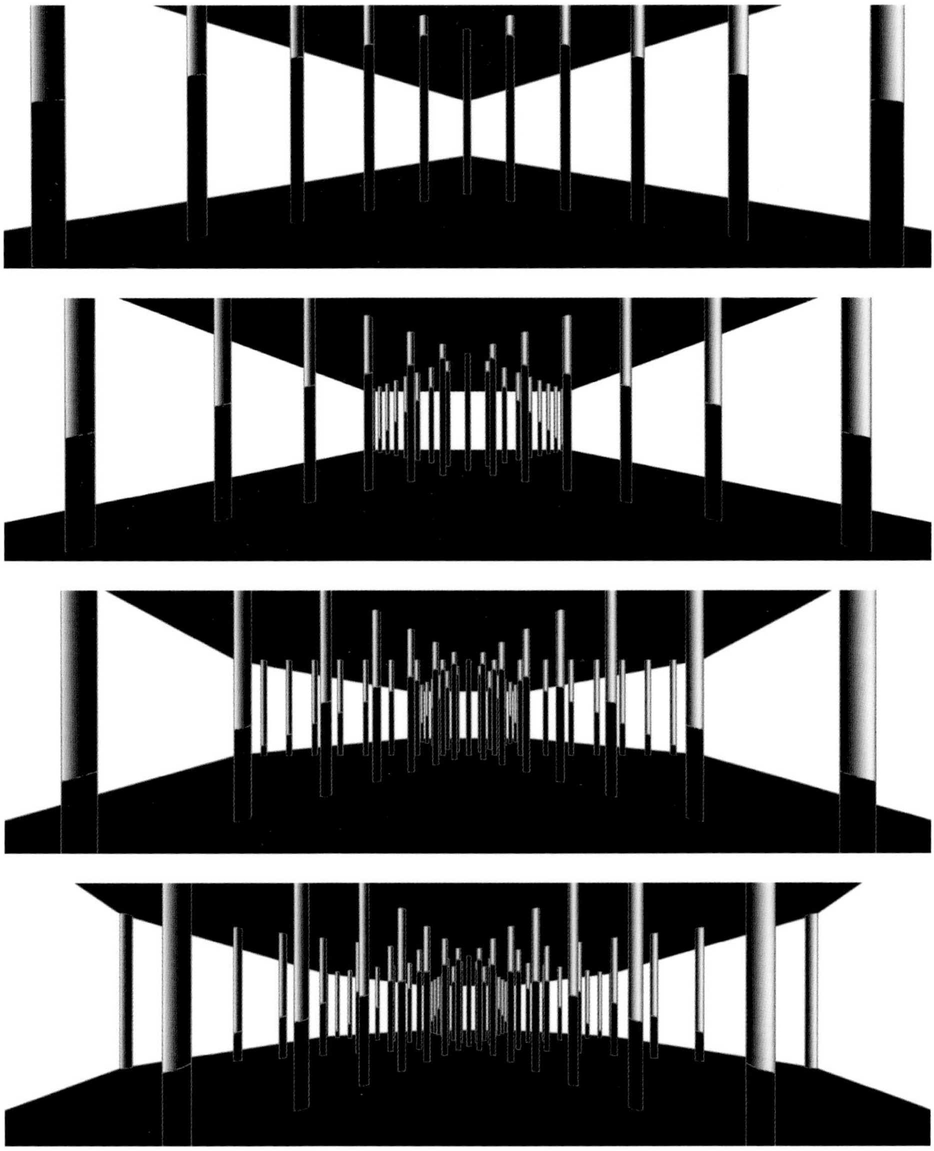

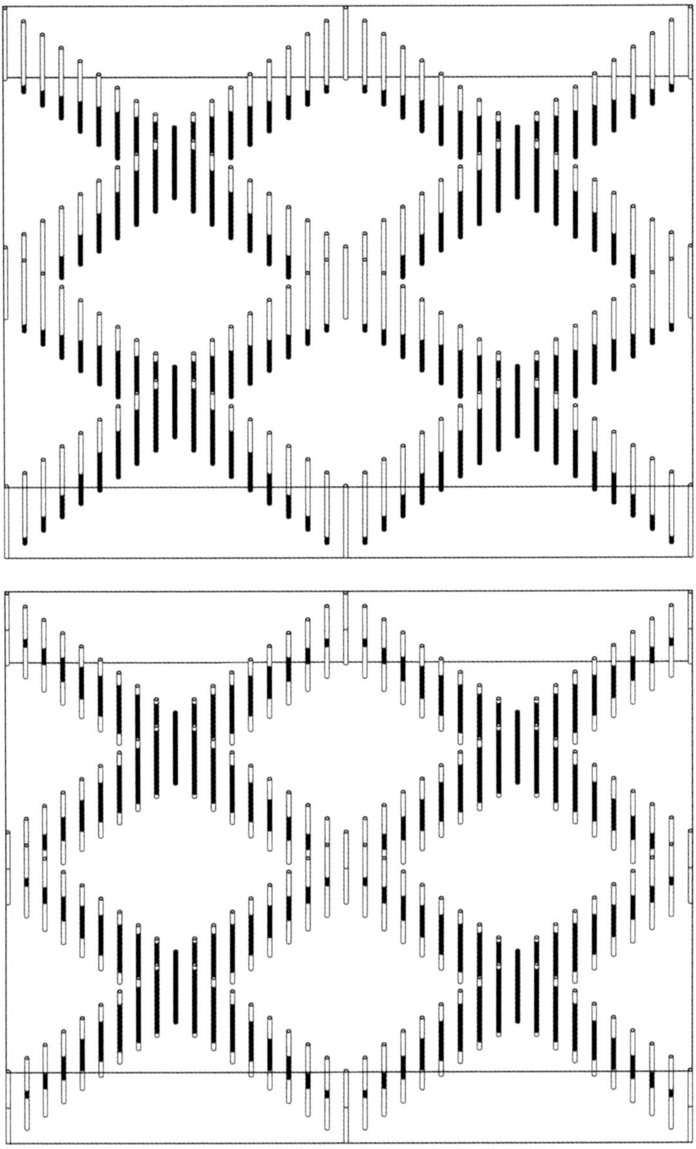

AGGREGATION OF MULTIPLE ZONES

The grouping of multiple zones produces a Concrete Deserta: an immesurable and continuous field of spatial intensities.

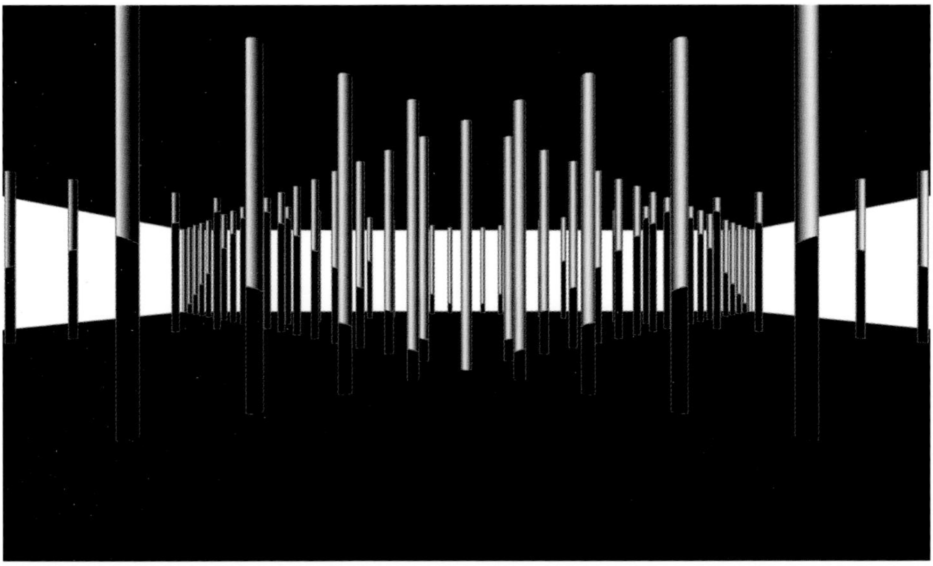

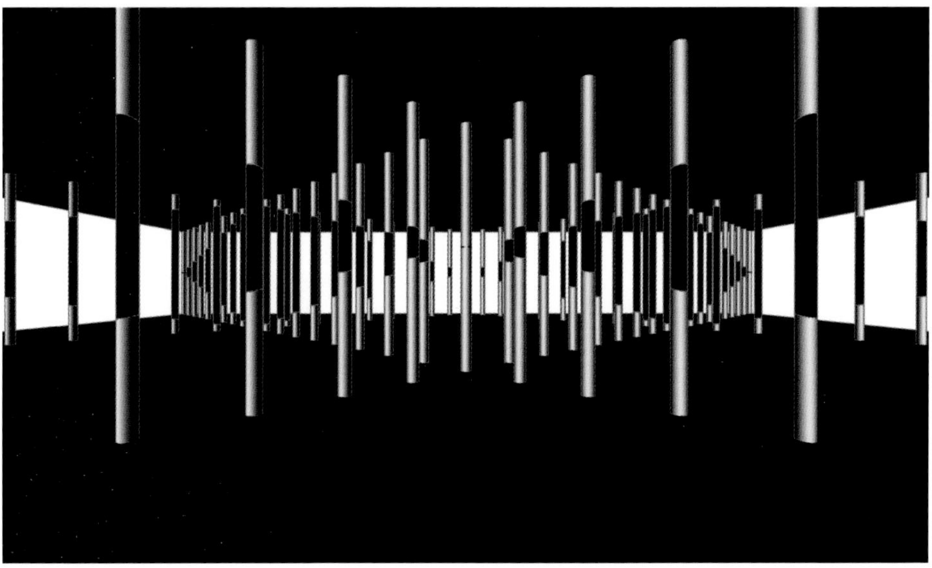

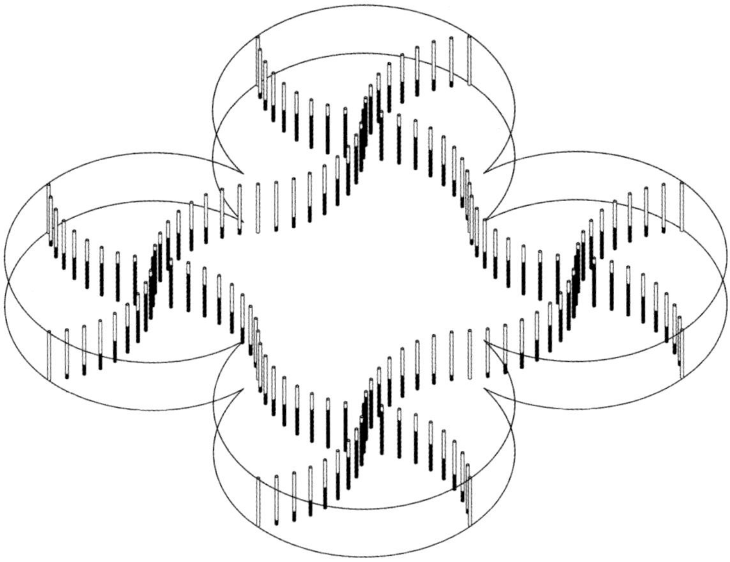

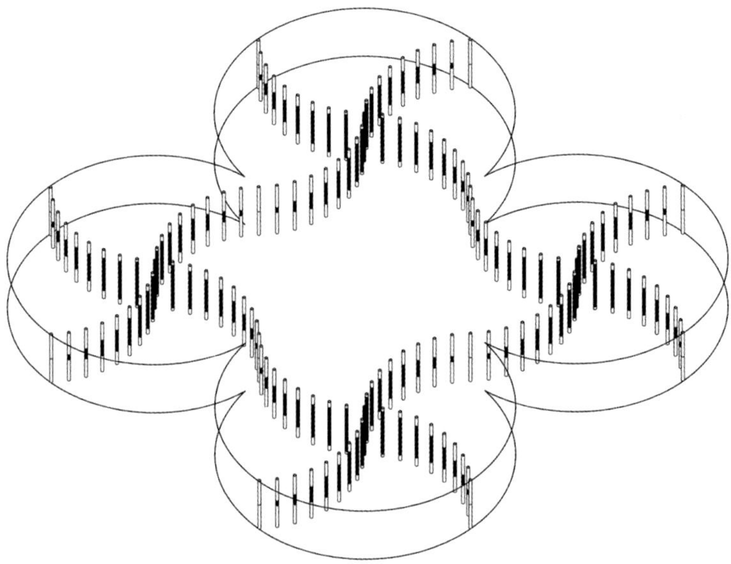

AGGREGATION OF MULTIPLE ZONES

Grouping of four circular zones.

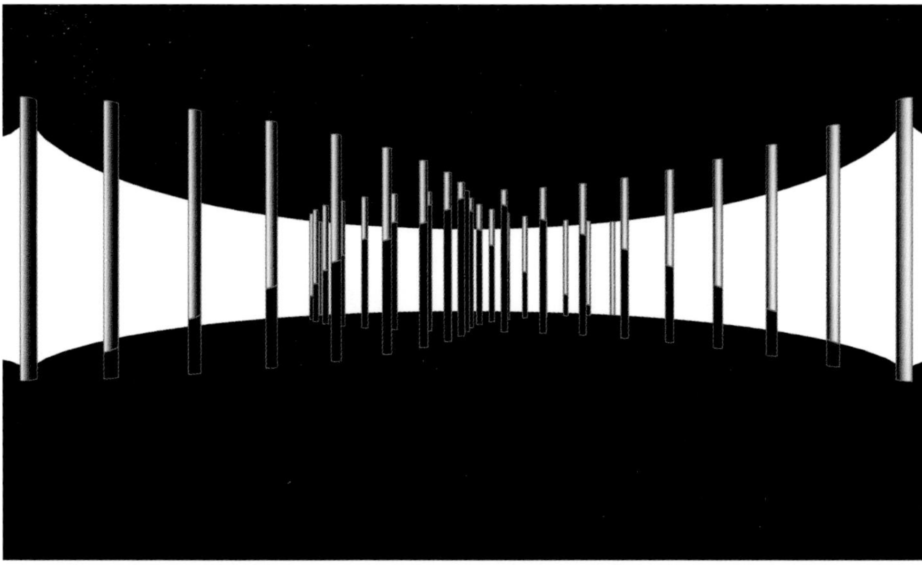

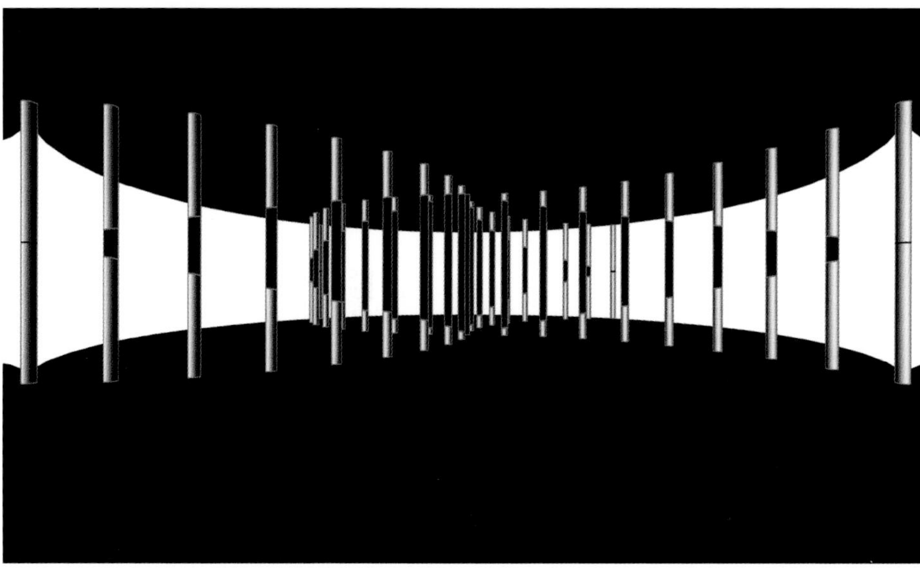

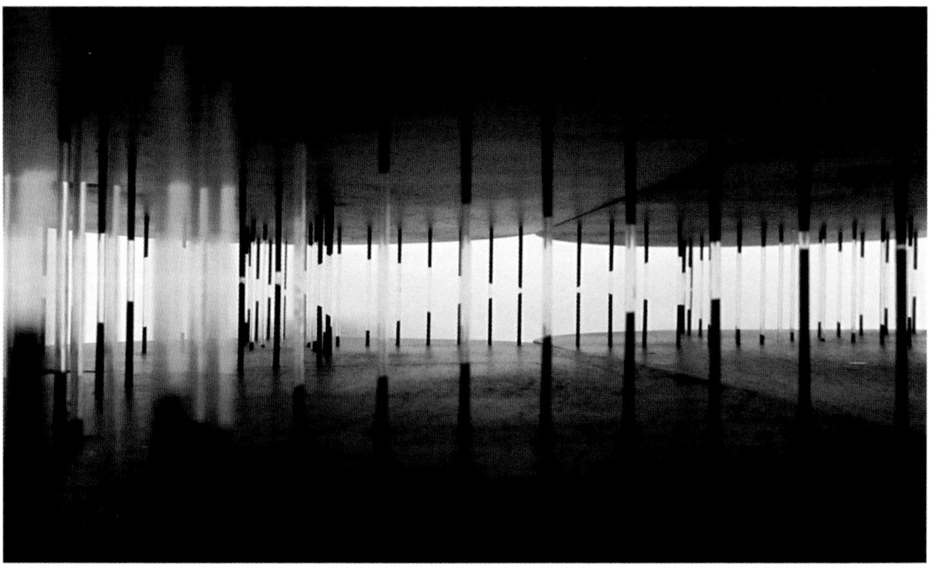

INTERIOR IMAGES OF A CONCRETE DESERTA

Models by Wesley Lam and Stephen Shchurowsky.

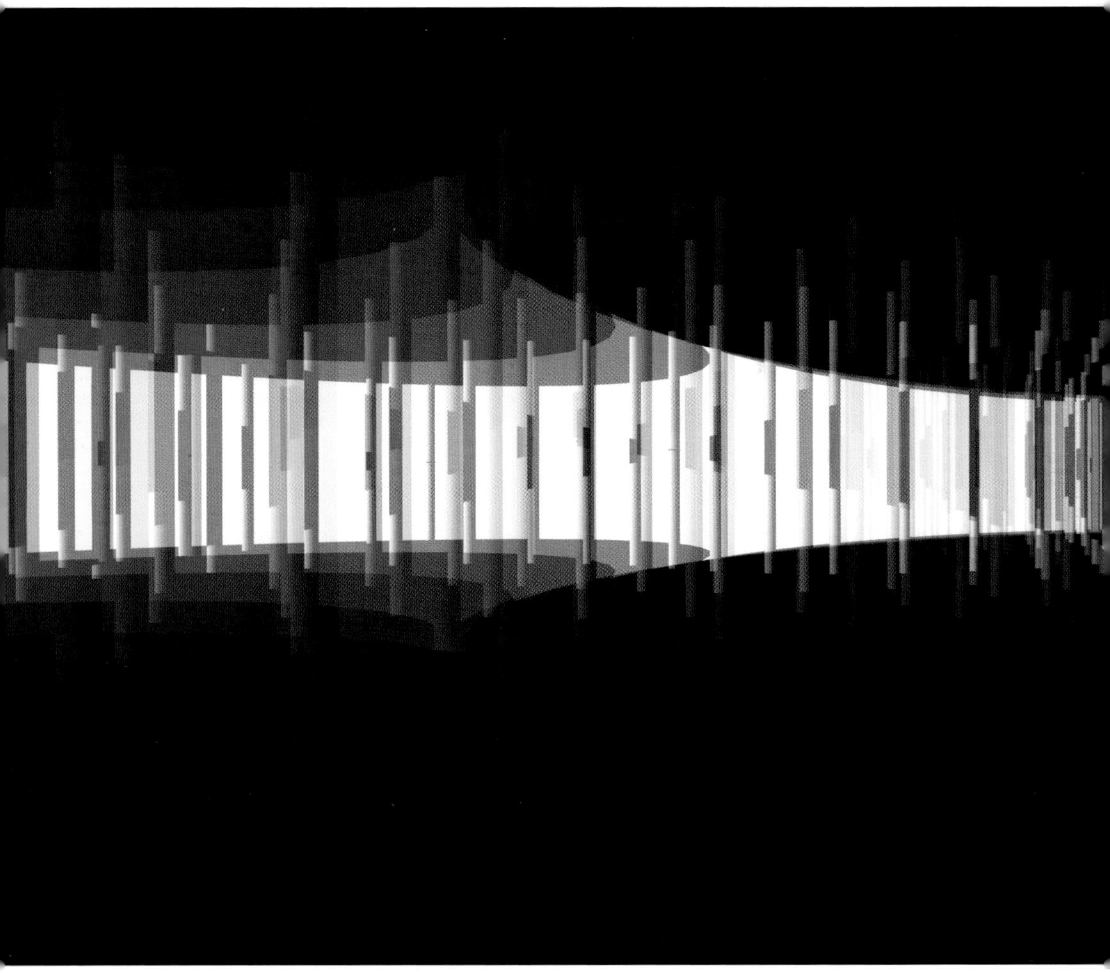

PERCEPTION OF A ZONE OF INTENSITY

Drawing represents a circular Concrete Deserta as experienced by a stroll through the space.

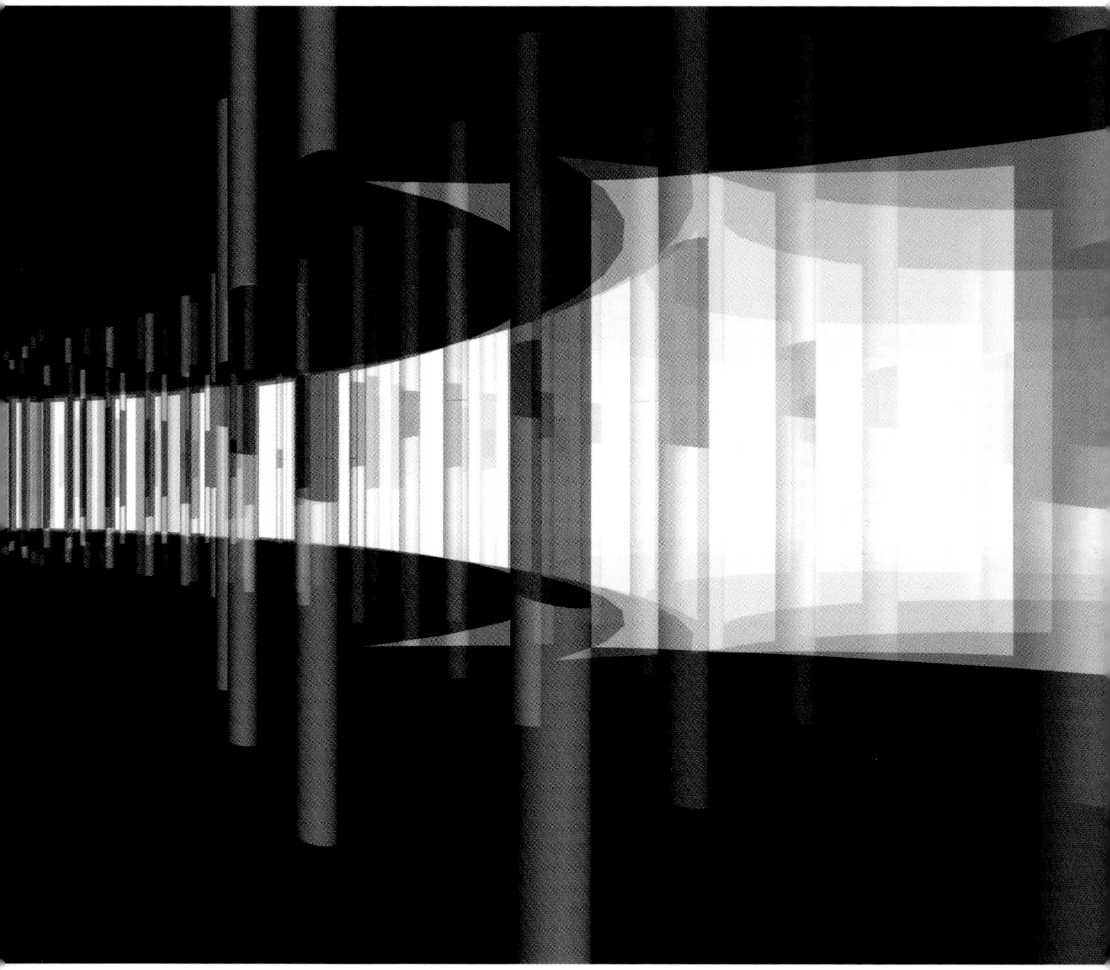

Bethune Hall interior
Image courtesy University Archives
State University of New York at Buffalo

Now you are ready to go.

Begin by following the signs of Century Boulevard; so that you can concentrate fully on your driving, switch off the guidance system when you hear the tone.

Have a nice day, and here comes the switch off tone.

Voice over from the fake audio city tour Baeda Kar Vistitor Guidance System in *Reyner Banham Loves L.A.* (BBC documentary, 1972), min 1.23.

ARCHITECTS [ENABLERS, ICONOGRAPHERS AND AGITATORS], CITIZENS OF THE WORLD, DOUBT! [OR HOW TO BECOME A UTOPIANIZER]

EVA FRANCH I. GILABERT

Today, architecture serves, provides and fulfills the needs and expectations of bodies and users in cultural and/or material terms. Within this mode of architectural consumption three models of architect can be identified: the enabler, the iconographer and the agitator.

The enabler, with more or less cynic or cool arguments, limits his/her duty or creative task to accommodate the multiplicities of projected desires with no further questioning on the origin or nature of the problem posed. With this position, the enabler is identical to the dictator: both have as clients ideological constructions and their intellectual game becomes a meta-discourse inside their constraints (technical, functional, geometrical, cultural, environmental, social, political, moral and in more general or perverse terms "disciplinary").

On the other hand, the iconographer, immersed in a drama of signification and communication, plays the frustrating game of difference and sameness in the search for a frozen firework that while desiring to be in the realm of the sublime is in the fringe of the banal without ever achieving, even if provocative, the realm of the revolutionary.

The third case, the agitator, is the avant-garde architect, disturbed, molested and in constant revolution against everything and all. The agitator plays the game of "resistance" and wants to be the infant terrible whose parents (the enabler and the iconographer), often in a complicated relationship, need to be killed in an act of terrorism or genealogical war.

With these three categories, users can fulfill all of their expectations of service and spectacle and architects can find their jobs: the enabler constructs spaces (of habitation or discourse), the iconographer constructs images (consumable) and the agitator constructs events (memorable).

The "closure of the situations" and the "closure of the responses" give immense conditions of possibility. However, the whole process and the resulting architectural landscape appear embedded in an atmosphere of irrelevance and banality in social, political and cultural terms. Why? Our society is highly immersed in a consumer "culture" where desires and users are being constructed through marketing, where play no longer equals freedom but numbness, and where politics and wars do not stand behind democracy (if they ever did) and global neoliberalism has left the individual without a collective sphere of discussion. Users with their architects have become passive workers of a system that produces capital through their exchange.

Professionalized attitudes, catalogued expectations, touristic and voyeuristic intellectual and pragmatic approaches define our current situation. For this, the degree of alienation that users and architects carry without awareness needs to be superseded by a new attitude and with it, a new architecture.

In this very specific moment there is the need to introduce a fourth type, a highly disregarded one, sometimes confused for an enabler or a dictator, sometimes for an iconographer and sometimes for an agitator, and certainly, it has similarities with all of them: the utopianizer.

What differentiates the utopianizer from the ideological constructions of his/her colleagues is his/her ability to doubt. The utopianizer is an architect that doubts the current structures of power and provides and envisions a process, a path, a vector of desire and will towards a place from where to establish a new paradigm. The utopianizer is an architect between a non desirable condition and a possible future, it constructs its path while it engages a process of separation and doubt. For this, in a time where social, political and ideological agendas seem to have reached a level of stagnation vis-a-vis the emergence of possible futures, doubt, in its generative sense, is a mode -and a mood- of inquiry that is necessary to be addressed.

In Western societies, to doubt has been culturally rendered as a non-productive activity. The hesitant walker in the crowded sidewalk, the one who doubts, impedes the immense flow of the crowd. Not as a strategy of resistance, already assimilated in the structures of power, but of conscious action, to doubt allows us to question and thus generate new trajectories and paths to explore cities and thoughts.

Twentieth century architecture has had plenty of doubts. The certainties of high-modernism were followed by an amalgam of strategies of doubt in principle from postmodern ironies to deconstructive fragments passing by the doubts as finale of the avant-gardes. However, the disciplinary inquiry resided in the realm of the Cartesian certainty or the Cartesian doubt (grounded altogether in a constant oblivion of the senses and the social realm) and with it we all received the prescribed diseases, doctors and medicines: the formalist anxieties, the critical and post-critical therapies and recently the Projective-Zacs, and there we are, or so it seems.

The utopinizer, with his/her architecture as doubt proposes a methodological approach towards architectural production that tries to unveil sensual, cognitive and political histories of architecture in a turn from a rhetoric of representation and consumption towards a production of sensation and creative action.

Acknowledging that the sensed environment has not been monopolized by canonized realms, the new materials to construct are to be found in the multiplicity of sensorial modalities. An alienated architecture of non-sense will be superseded by a sensed architecture able to trigger new and unexpected reactions; it will provide atmospheres of surprise, of sensual encounter and ideological disruptions where political, social and cultural relationships between users can emerge in a conscious and visceral condition.

For this, the question each architect, each utopianizer, needs to formulate now in political, social and conceptual terms is: what architectural doubt am I going to build today?

To ask a question though, does not necessary presuppose an answer, but a method of action and inquiry. A method is a path towards an unknown destination.

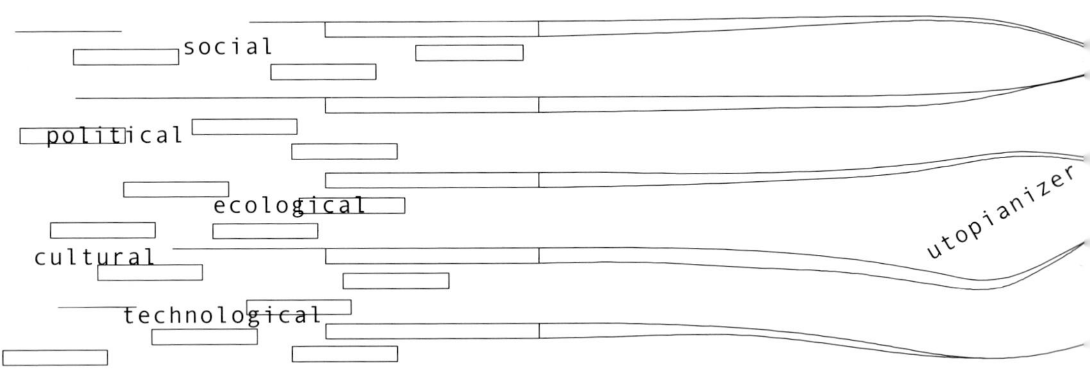

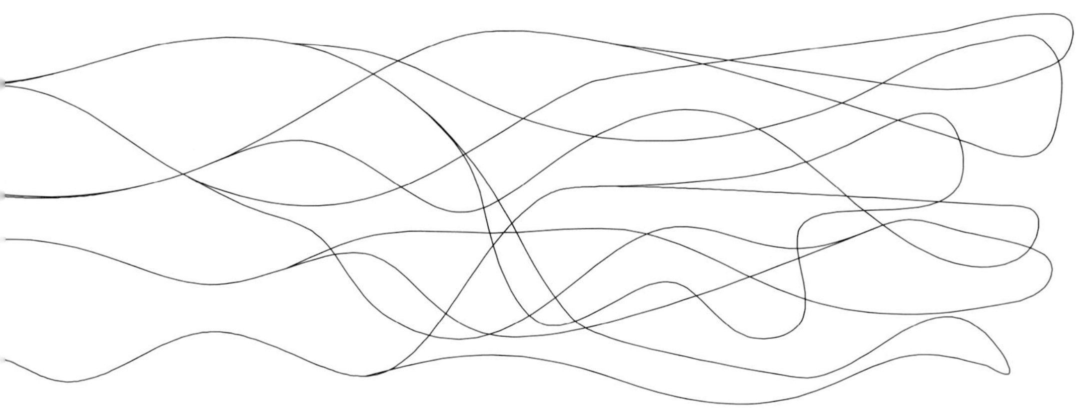

UTOPIANIZING

Chronological image from left [past] to right [future] of the schims of practice and thought.

1971

Los Angeles: The Architecture of Four Ecologies | Original Scale

50% Scale

1972

Learning from Las Vegas | Original Scale

It's a poor historian who finds any human artefact alien to his professional capacities, a poorer one who cannot find new bottles for new wine.

Peter Reyner Banham, *Los Angeles: The Architecture of Four Ecologies* (New York: Harper and Row, 1971), 21.

PUBLISHING PRACTICES
MICHAEL KUBO

Since the advent of print culture, the practice of architecture has been closely related to the practice of publishing by architects. If it is by now taken for granted that architectural projects operate discursively as well as spatially, publishing has been an important means by which architects have shaped discursive contexts for producing, receiving, and interpreting architectural work. The most prominent architects in the field have often been its most prolific publishers. They have acted as authors (of monographs, manifestoes, histories, treatises, lectures, charters, pamphlets, transcripts, catalogues), editors (of magazines, journals, and other serial formats), and curators (not just of exhibitions but of networks for producing and disseminating published work including publishing houses, imprints, groups, conferences, meetings). Certain architects have regarded the design process itself as a form of editing; some have drawn on prior experience in fields like journalism, filmmaking, and graphic design in their later architectural work. All of these roles have intersected with those of historians, theorists, and critics, who have engaged the discourse of the field from their own disciplinary perspectives.

How many architecture-related books do you buy in an average year?

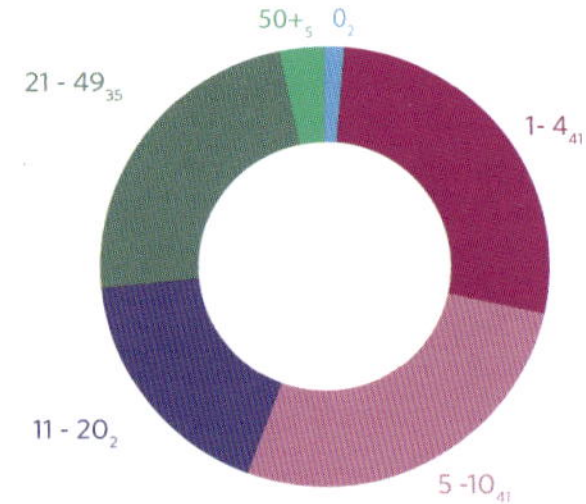

How many architecture-related books do you own?

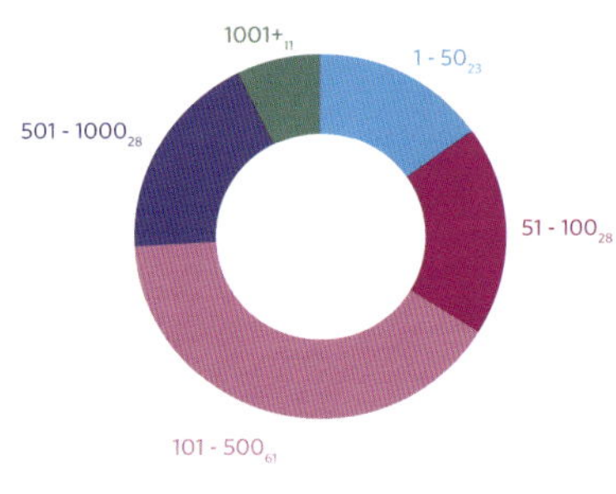

Architects have increasingly come to see books as strategic tools in their disciplinary arsenal, capable of producing effects very different from those of more traditional forms of production. The relationship between publishing and building has often been exploited as a critical double form of architectural practice, an interweaving of two strands of work that are typically assumed to mirror each other, but which often reveal a provocative (and in many cases deliberate) misalignment. Instead of regarding publishing as merely subsidiary to 'practice'—understood to mean the production of buildings—the most prominent architects and critics have exploited the tactical differences between books and buildings, engaging with both as distinct but related kinds of discursive practice. In this history publishing appears as an alternative form of architecture, one that is frequently more agile than other forms of practice more typically understood as architectural.[1]

Where do you get architectural information from these days?

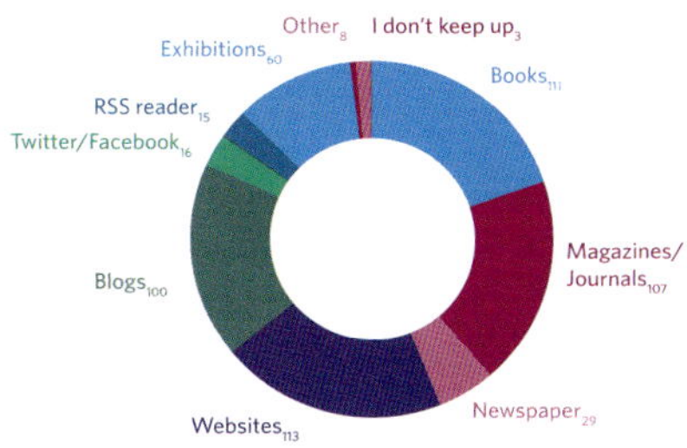

Where do you typically buy architecture books?

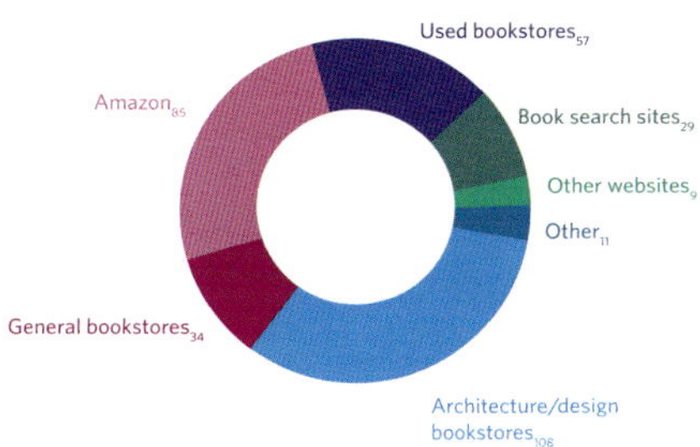

The Publishing Practices project traces the history and influence of architectural publishing as an operative device, through an examination of books produced by architects and authors in the past century. Case studies present the origins, composition, and after-products of ten influential architecture books, each one representative of a particular era of architectural production and a specific attitude towards the role and effects of publishing by its practitioners. Beyond providing a particular picture of twentieth-century architecture as told through its publications, the case studies reveal a legacy of reformatting certain privileged genres of the twentieth-century architectural book: the manifesto, the monograph, and the history.[2]

The manifesto is often seen as being closest to the traditional idea of a guide for practice. It is by definition polemical, outlining a theory intended to be projected onto the field, in order to legitimize, instruct, or critique particular forms of production. Its lineage begins with the prototypical example of the twentieth-century architectural manifesto, Le Corbusier's *Vers une Architecture* (1923), and is followed by a series of inversions and revisions to the form, from the 'gentle' manifesto—Robert Venturi's *Complexity and Contradiction in Architecture* (1966)—to the 'retroactive' manifesto—Rem Koolhaas's *Delirious New York* (1978).[3] A related genre, also represented here, could be called the 'city as manifesto'. The form took shape in the 1970s in the turn towards the existing city as an object of study, poised halfway between urban history and the traditional mode of the theoretical treatise. It uses the identification of a specific urban condition—its representation to architects, an account of its potentials, and/or a deliberate reframing of its history—as a manifesto for rethinking architectural and urban practices in the present. Its foundational examples include Reyner Banham's *Los Angeles: The Architecture of Four Ecologies* (1971), Robert Venturi, Denise Scott Brown and Steven Izenour's *Learning From Las Vegas*[4] (1972), and again *Delirious New York*, which is thus one of the first examples of a new genre and an explicit reformatting of an existing (Corbusian) precedent.[5]

For these authors the manifesto has not been simply reducible to a guide. Though polemicism is part of its strategic mode of operation, the manifesto is not subordinate to or exclusively directed toward practice. Rather, its role is often to create a context in which other forms of (architectural) production can be interpreted, just as buildings create a discursive context in which writing and publishing practices (often by the same authors) can be received in turn. Neither is merely a demonstration of, or prescription for, the other.

Did books play an important role in your studio work?

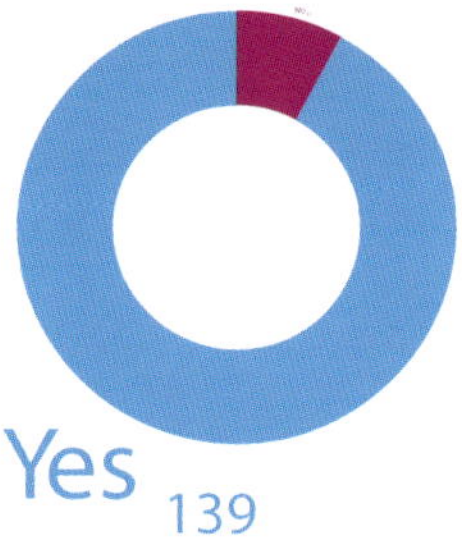

A second privileged form of the twentieth-century architecture book is the monograph. It attempts to frame a body of work as constituting an agenda through practice, whereas in the manifesto agendas are framed first through theoretical or polemical statements. The monograph as a form is again initially dominated by the example of Le Corbusier, in the exhaustive form of his *Œvre Complete*, published in eight volumes from 1929 to 1965. The subsequent revisions to the genre have been innumerable. These include the appearance of projects at the end of a manifesto to demonstrate that through theory 'an architectural discovery has taken place'[6] (in *Complexity and Contradiction in Architecture*, and, less well remembered today, in the first edition of *Learning From Las Vegas*; the same method is reprised in fictional form in *Delirious New York*). Peter Eisenman's *Houses of Cards* (1987) mixes the processes of writing, drawing, and building (along with building as drawing, drawing as writing, writing as building...) into an idea of the monograph as a conceptual construct, a form of architecture in itself. The series reached an apotheosis in the explosive *S,M,L,XL* (1995) by Rem Koolhaas and Bruce Mau, a promiscuous fusion of monograph and manifesto whose scale and graphic complexity both triggered a new genre of book and marked a provisional terminus of the old.[7]

The last genre of book included here is the polemical or operative history. Polemical histories attempt to reconstruct the past—to lay out the 'canon' of architects and projects anew—to provide a historical framework for understanding and legitimizing particular ways of working in the present. Examples range from the universalizing ambition of Sigfried Giedion's *Space, Time and Architecture* (1941), which aimed to provide (and was largely taken as) the official history of the modern movement in architecture, to the more intimate (and certainly more humble) approach of the personal scrapbook of sources, as in Alison and Peter Smithson's *The Heroic Period of Modern Architecture* (1965).

A word needs to be said about the choice of case studies in Publishing Practices as a particular 'canon' of books within the architectural field. How do we define the term 'canonical'? According to one argument (often made by those invested in the idea of a canon as something that needs to be 'defended'), the identification of certain works as canonical is essential to the very idea of architecture as a discipline. The fact of having and naming a shared canon—of being able to label certain works as 'canonical'—corresponds to architecture's self-identification as a distinct discipline, well defined unto itself (and not, for example, simply a subset of other practices). That is, if architecture is held to be a discipline, it must have a canon. In this formulation, the discipline does not simply constitute its canon; it could be said equally that the canon constitutes a discipline. An extreme version of this argument would be the exclusionary claim that, as an architect, one is not simply expected to be familiar with these books; rather, if one does not know the canon, one is not an architect. In this view, far from being an arbitrary designation assigned to works after the fact, the identification of canonical books is part and parcel of the constitution of the discipline itself.

While the above may sound like an outmoded definition, this idea of canonicity has informed the production of architecture books for at least the last century. Despite the problems in talking about architecture as a well-defined 'discipline', and whatever other forms of media have been produced and circulated in and around architectural practice, the continued agility and durability of the book has made it a privileged format for architects hoping to construct this canonicity, for both their books and themselves. The issue resurfaces today when even the newest and supposedly most agile forms of media, such as blogs and websites, still aspire to canonicity—to engage with the traditionally canonical modes of architectural discourse or become canonical themselves—by adopting the privileged form of the book.[8]

Rather than speaking in terms of disciplinarity—with all the boundaries and exclusions that term implies—the selection of case studies in "Pubishing Practices" has relied on thinking about architecture as a field of cultural production, in which publishing is one among many modes of practice, different from but no less important in its operation than the production of buildings.[9] In this field, both publishing and building practices have been equally necessary in creating the possibility for discursive modes of operation in architecture.[10] A 'canonical' project (if we still allow ourselves to use the term) in this view would be one in which a discursive project is most clearly revealed in the work's totality as a textual object—a careful and deliberate construction of format, layout, images, and words—in relation to other discursive practices. A list of canonical works defined this way might then correspond more closely to those works that have been the most instrumental in their operation. These are works that one could expect to find consistently across the major sites of architectural production, transmission, and reception at a given historical moment, as forms of shared knowledge and practice within the field. This definition of canonicity is not an ahistorical judgment of quality but an assessment of a work's efficacy as a discursive practice within its particular historical and productive context.

Did you read books primarily through seminars and other non-studio work?

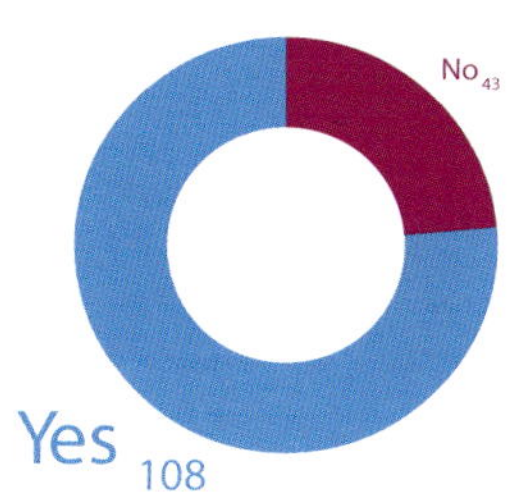

(Previous Page, Above) Responses to survey on books and their influence, 2009. Graphic design: Chris Grimley.

To get at this question of efficacy, one has to study not only the production of architectural books but also their reception and impact within the field, which is often very different from their intended agendas. Beyond the study of publishing as an operative practice (and its strategic role for its practitioners), "Publishing Practices" involved a survey of over 500 practitioners, educators, and students to gauge the impact of publications (whether architectural or otherwise) on those trained in the architectural field. The survey responses and the data graphics that were produced from them led to certain provisional conclusions about the instrumentality and efficacy of architectural books. On the simplest level, the books that were listed most frequently by survey participants included five out of the ten case studies already chosen—*S,M,L,XL, Delirious New York, Complexity and*

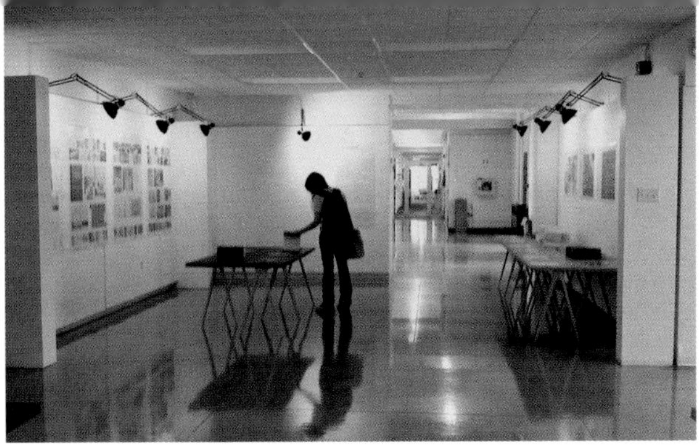

Contradiction in Architecture, Learning From Las Vegas, and Vers une Architecture—confirming the impact of those works. On the other hand, their listing was consistent across the different ages, places and periods of education, and current practices of the respondents, from those trained in the 1960s until the present. Surprisingly, there were no peaks of influence for these books around the moment of their publication or for those trained in particular eras. Indeed, their consistent appearance in the lists of even the most recent students reveals the continuing influence of these publications up to the present, despite radical changes in the production and dissemination of both architecture and books and the emergence of other, competing forms of media in the digital era.

As the last member of this chronology, the survey raised the particular question of whether *S,M,L,XL* may stand as the final, definitive example of the canonical book. With its dramatic appearance at a moment of confluence between new modes of production, the rising cultural status of the architect, the first impacts of globalization on architectural and publishing practices, and the increasing influence of theory—but before a more pronounced split between history/theory and practice as increasingly separate disciplines catering to different audiences, the over-proliferation of architectural publishing, and the rise of digital media that would alter the production and reception of the book after the 1990s—its discursive impact may be impossible to replicate, as the reflection of a unique confluence of historical factors. No publication emerged from the survey as a likely candidate for the 'next' canonical book; it remains to be seen whether there will be one again, or whether the idea of the canonical and the role of publishing among other practices have undergone a definitive change in the meantime.

(Top) Publishing Practices exhibition, University at Buffalo, May 2009. (Bottom) Publishing Practices exhibition, pinkcomma gallery, Boston, October 2009. (Right) Publishing Practices roundtable, University at Buffalo, May 2009.

NOTES:

1 There has been a resurgence of interest in publishing practices in architecture, particularly for magazines and journals and more recently for the book. An initial example of this interest was *Clip/Stamp/Fold: The Radical Architecture of Little Magazines 196X–197X*, the collaborative research of Beatriz Colomina and Ph.D. students at Princeton, which was initially exhibited at the Storefront for Art and Architecture in New York in November 2006. A more recent example is Mimi Zeiger's exhibition A Few Zines: Dispatches from the Edge of Architectural Production, held at Studio X in New York in January 2009 and later in Boston. In the past three years alone, seminars on publishing and discursive practice in schools of architecture have been taught by (among others) Jeannie Kim at Columbia, Ana Miljacki at Columbia and MIT, Michael Kubo in Buffalo, Lars Müller at Harvard, Luke Bulman at Yale, and Elite Kedan at Florida International University. The recent formation of the Master of Science in Critical, Curatorial, and Conceptual Practices (CCCP) at Columbia under Felicity Scott confirms this new interest to introduce publishing practices and their histories more fully into the pedagogy of architecture.

2 Of the case studies presented here, *Vers une Architecture, Learning From Las Vegas, Delirious New York, and S,M,L,XL* are examples of canonical books that have recently undergone a more comprehensive documentation of their origins, processes of production, agendas, and modes of operation. Many of the images included in the timeline are taken from these sources, which are listed in the notes that follow.

3 For *Vers une Architecture*, see Jean Louis-Cohen, ed., *Towards an Architecture* (Los Angeles: Getty Instititute, 2007), which provides a new translation by John Goodman and a new layout that restore both the language and the design schema of the original. For Le Corbusier's publishing practice more generally, see Catherine de Smet, *Le Corbusier: Architect of Books* (Basel: Lars Muller, 2006). For *Delirious New York*, see Beatriz Colomina's separate interviews with Rem Koolhaas, in *El Croquis* 134/135 (2007), and Madelon Vriesendorp, in Shumon Basar and Stephen Trüby, eds., *The World of Madelon Vriesendorp* (London: Architectural Association, 2008). For Koolhaas's background in journalism and filmmaking prior to studying architecture, see Bart Lootsma, *'Now Switch off the Sound and Reverse the Film; Koolhaas, Constant, and Dutch Culture in the 1960s'*, in Jennifer Sigler, ed., *Hunch 1* (1999).

4 For *Learning From Las Vegas*, see Aron Vinegar, *I Am a Monument: On Learning From Las Vegas* (Cambridge: MIT Press, 2008); Vinegar and Michael J. Golec, eds., *Relearning From Las Vegas* (Minneapolis: University of Minnesota, 2008); Kester Rattenbury and Samantha Hardingham, eds., *SuperCrit #2—Robert Venturi and Denise Scott Brown: Learning From Las Vegas* (London: Routledge, 2007); and Hilar Stadler and Martino Stierli, eds., *Las Vegas Studio* (Zurich: Scheidegger and Spiess, 2009).

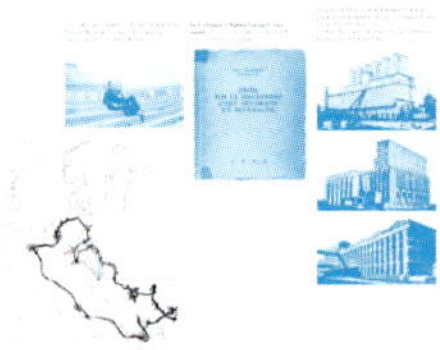

5 Koolhaas has placed Venturi and Scott Brown within this shift in genres and situated his own subsequent publishing practice in terms of that shift. In an interview of the pair conducted with Hans Ulrich Obrist in 2000, *Complexity and Contradiction in Architecture* is described as the 'last manifesto' in architecture; afterwards, Koolhaas claims, there are 'only books about the city that imply manifestoes.' The subsequent examples he cites of this new genre—works on New York, Los Angeles, Singapore, and Lagos—are essentially a list of his own later writings, with Banham's *Los Angeles: The Architecture of Four Ecologies* (which in fact predated the publication of *Learning From Las Vegas*, though not the Yale studio on which it was based) arguably acting as a stand-in for his own writings on other dispersed U.S. cities like Atlanta and Houston. See '*Relearning From Las Vegas*,' in Chung, Inaba, Koolhaas, and Leong, eds., *The Harvard Design School Guide to Shopping* (Cologne: Taschen, 2001).

6 Thanks to Enrique Walker for this formulation.

7 For *S,M,L,XL*, see Gabriele Mastrigli, "*The Last Bastion of Architecture*," *Log 7 (Winter/Spring 2006)*, and Brendan McGetrick's recent interview with Jennifer Sigler, the editor of *S,M,L,XL*, in Domus China (http://www.brendanmcgetrick.com/blog/2009/10/01/editalk-with-jen-sigler/). The images included in the timeline of archival materials from the production of *S,M,L,XL* are taken with permission from Jennifer Sigler, from her lecture on the book's history at the Beyond Media '03 conference in Florence in October 2003.

8 For example, see Geoff Manaugh's blog, BLDGBLOG (http://bldgblog.blogspot.com/), contents from which have recently been published as *The BLDGBLOG Book* (San Francisco: Chronicle Books, 2009).

9 See Pierre Bourdieu, *The Field of Cultural Production* (New York: Columbia University Press, 1993).

10 Thanks to Michael Meredith for this formulation.

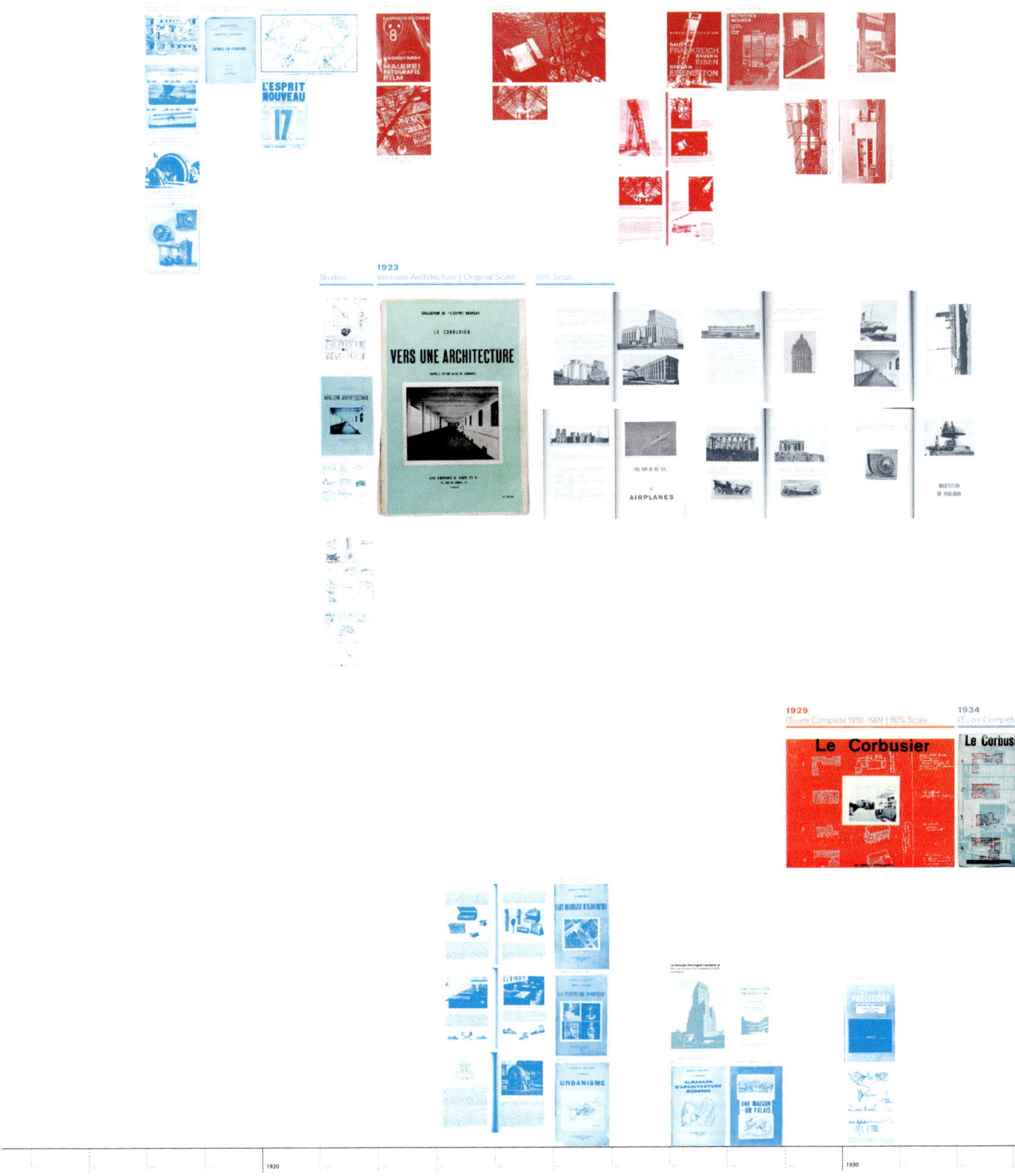

Timeline of case studies, their influences and after-products from 1910 to 2010. Graphic design: Chris Grimley.

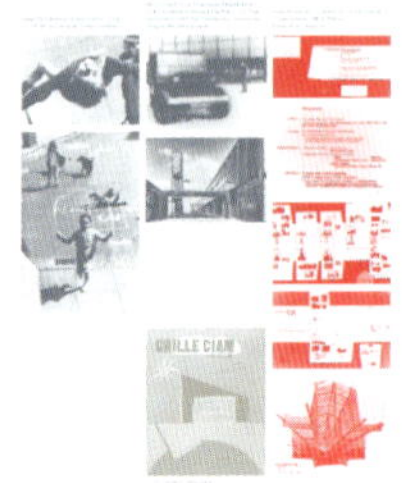

1937
Space, Time and Architecture | Original Scale

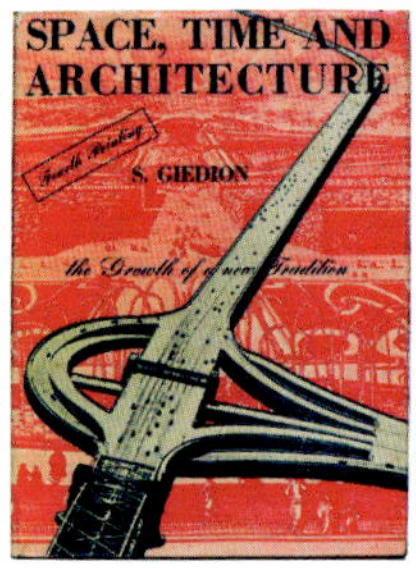

33% Scale

1949

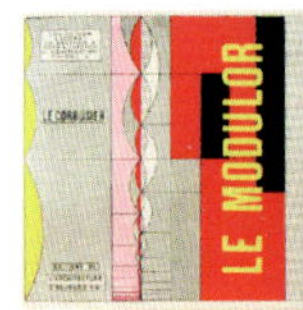

| 60% Scale

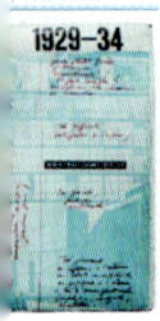

1934
Œuvre Complete 1934–1938 | 60% Scale

1946
Œuvre Complete 1938–1946 | 60% Scale

1940

1950

1966
Complexity and Contradiction in Architecture | Original Scale
33% Scale
Complexity and Contradiction in Architecture
Robert Venturi
1955
MODULOR 2
1965
The Heroic Period of Modern Architecture | Original Scale
33% Scale
THE HEROIC PERIOD OF MODERN ARCHITECTURE
1957
1965
Œuvre Complete 1957–1965 | 66% Scale
CORBUSIER
1946-52
Le Corbusier
Œuvre complète
1952–57
Le Corbusier 1957–65
THEORY DESIGN FIRST MACHINE AGE
LLV
team primer
1960
1970

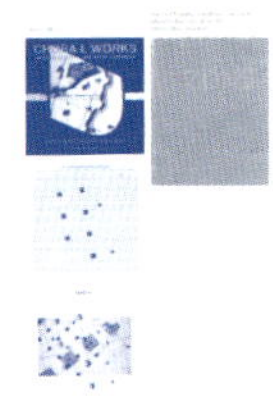
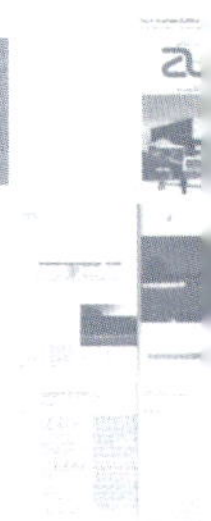

1971

Los Angeles: The Architecture of Four Ecologies | Original Scale

50% Scale

1978

Delirious New York | Original Scale

50% Scale

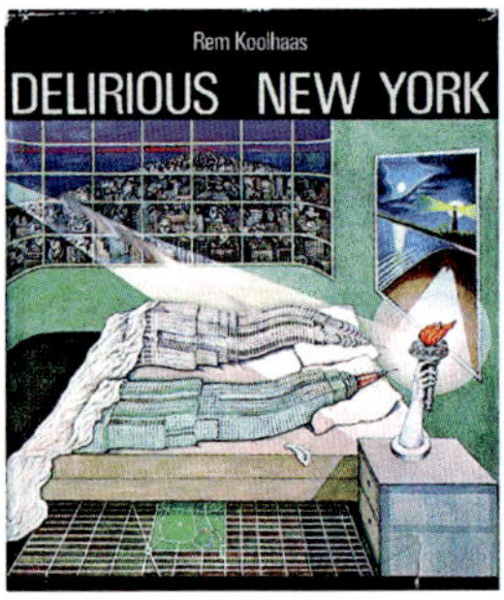

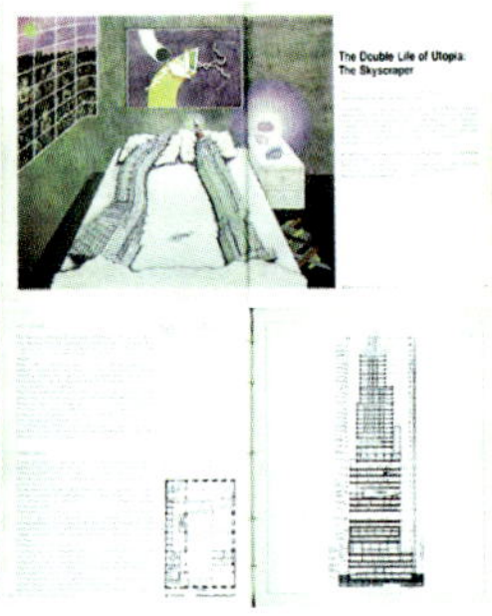

1972

Learning from Las Vegas | Original Scale

50% Scale

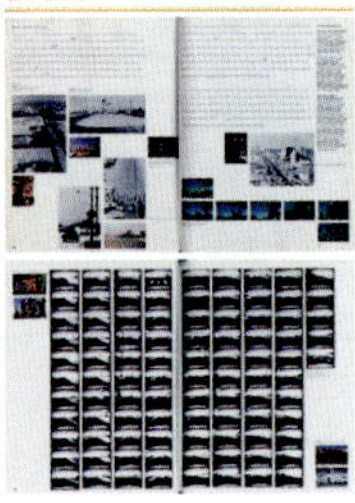

1987

Houses of Cards | Orig

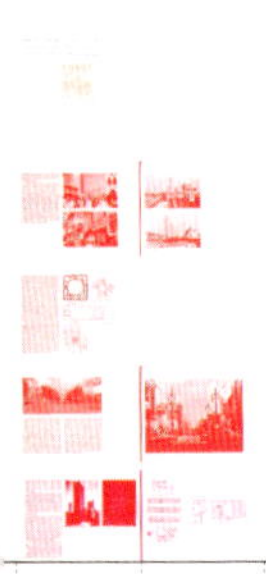

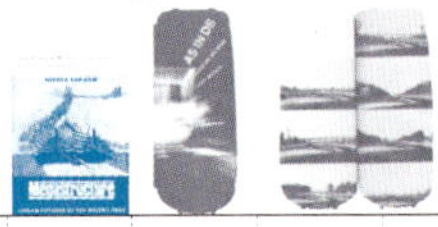

1980

OMA
6 PROJETS
1995
S,M,L,XL
O.M.A.
Rem Koolhaas
and Bruce Mau
010 Publishers
Good!
We weren't here
yesterday evening.
Now,
what did we do
yesterday evening?
Do?
AKTUELE SLIP-BOUTIQUE
50% Scale
HARVARD
GUIDE TO
SHOPPING
Content
1990
2000

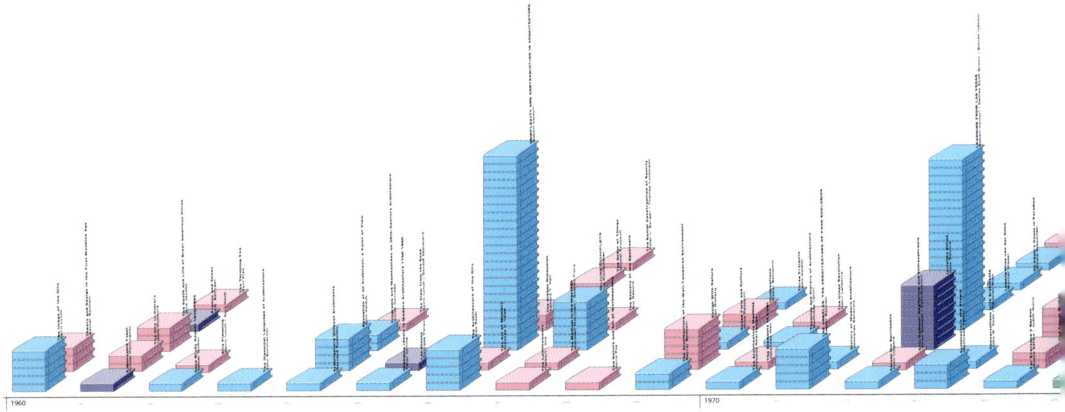
1960
1970

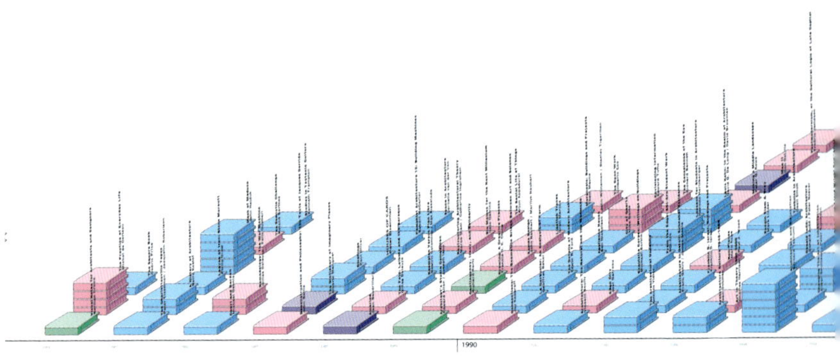
1990

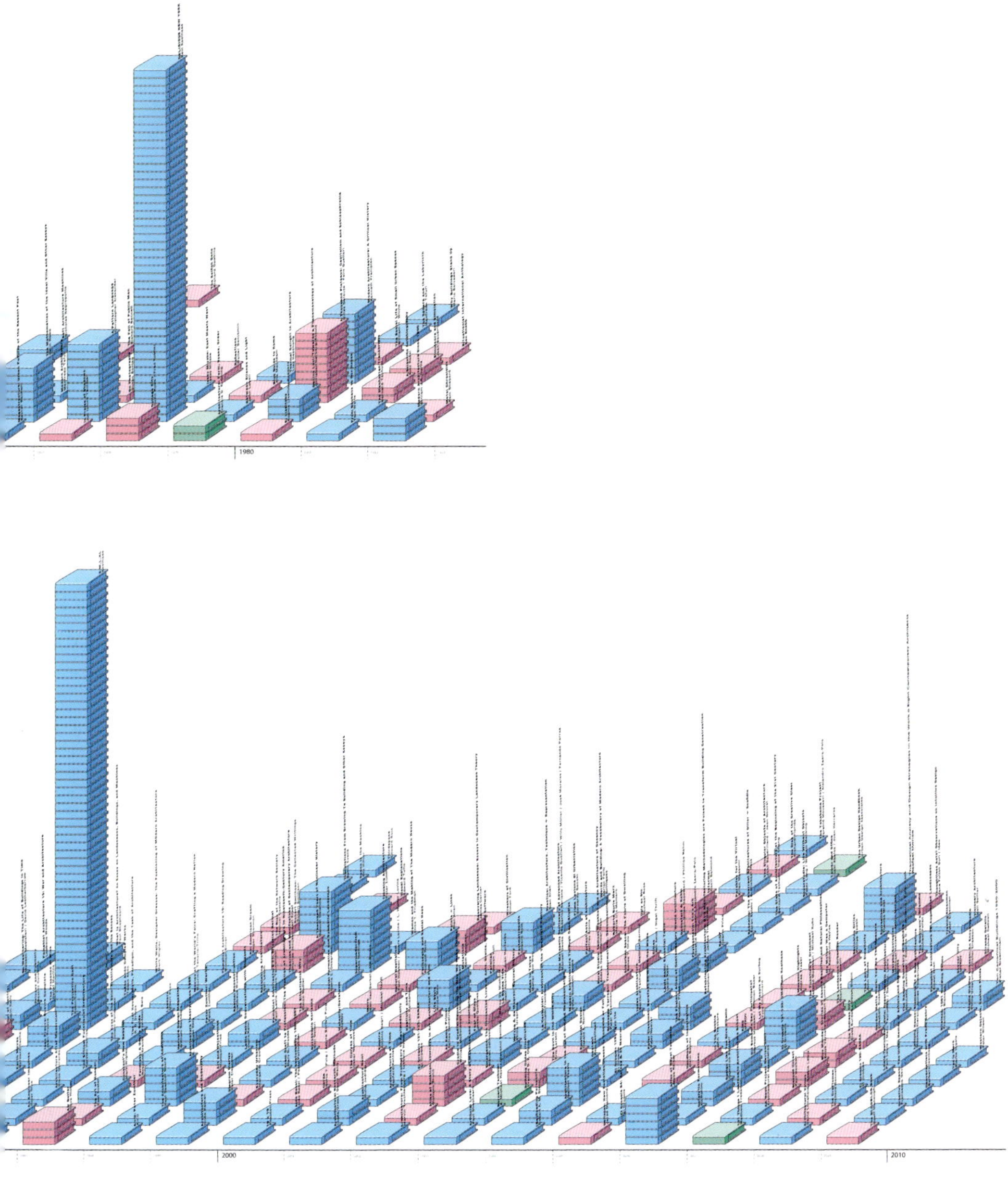

Timeline of books listed by survey respondents as most infuential from 1960 to 2010. Graphic design: Kyle Jonasen.

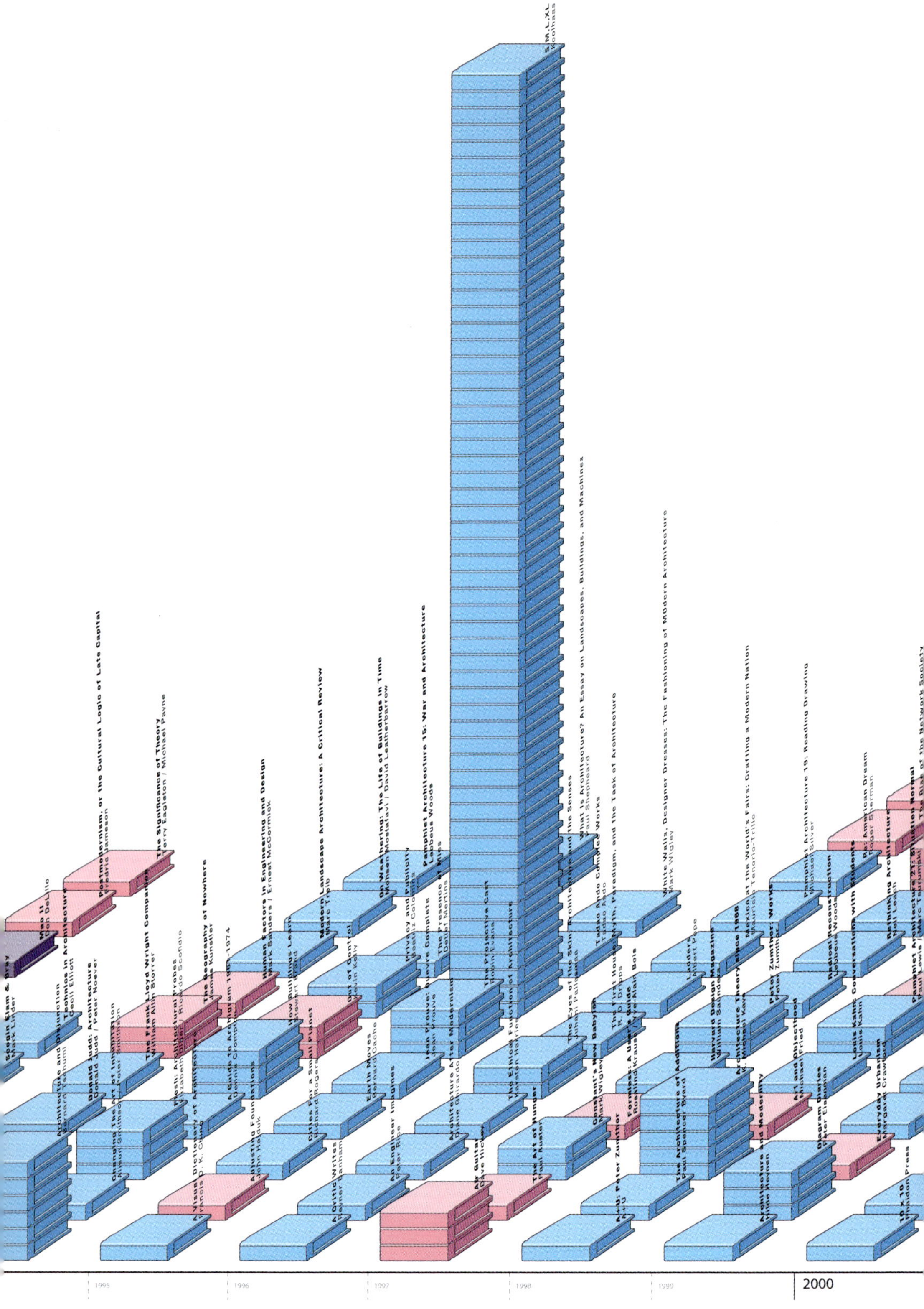

S,M,L,XL
Koolhaas
Postmodernism, or the Cultural Logic of Late Capital
Fredric Jameson
The Significance of Theory
Terry Eagleton / Michael Payne
Human Factors in Engineering and Design
Mark Sanders / Ernest McCormick
Modern Landscape Architecture: A Critical Review
Marc Treib
On Weathering: The Life of Buildings in Time
Mohsen Mostafavi / David Leatherbarrow
Pamphlet Architecture 15: War and Architecture
Lebbeus Woods
What Is Architecture? An Essay on Landscapes, Buildings, and Machines
Paul Shepheard
White Walls, Designer Dresses: The Fashioning of MOdern Architecture
Mark Wigley
Mexico at the World's Fairs: Crafting a Modern Nation
Mauricio Tenorio-Trillo
Pamphlet Architecture 19: Reading Drawing
Michael Silver
Mao II
Don DeLillo
Architecture and Disjunction
Bernard Tschumi
Tectonics in Architecture
Cecil Elliott
Donald Judd: Architecture
Peter Noever
Changing the Art of Inhabitation
Alison Smithson / Peter Smithson
The Frank Lloyd Wright Companion
William Allin Storrer
Flesh: Architectural Probes
Elizabeth Diller / Ricardo Scofidio
The Geography of Nowhere
James Kunstler
A Visual Dictionary of Architecture
Francis D. K. Ching
A Guide to Archigram 1961-1974
Dennis Crompton
Adjusting Foundations
John Hejduk
How Buildings Learn
Stewart Brand
Cities For a Small Planet
Richard Rogers
A Critic Writes
Reyner Banham
Out of Control
Kevin Kelly
Earth Moves
Bernard Cache
An Engineer Imagines
Peter Rice
Privacy and Publicity
Beatriz Colomina
Jean Prouvé
Jean Prouvé
Air Guitar
Dave Hickey
The Projective Cast
Robin Evans
The Ethical Function of Architecture
Karsten Harries
The Eyes of the Skin: Architecture and the Senses
Juhani Pallasmaa
Tadao Ando Complete Works
Tadao Ando
Constant's New Babylon
Mark Wigley
Formless: A User's Guide
Rosalind Krauss / Yve-Alain Bois
A+U: Peter Zumthor
A+U
The Architecture of Additions
Paul Spencer Byard
Ladders
Albert Pope
Architecture Theory since 1968
K. Michael Hays
Architecture and Modernity
Hilde Heynen
Peter Zumthor: Works
Peter Zumthor
Radical Reconstruction
Lebbeus Woods
Art and Objecthood
Michael Fried
Diagram Diaries
Peter Eisenman
Louis Kahn: Conversations with Students
Louis Kahn
Rethinking Architecture
Neil Leach
Everyday Urbanism
Margaret Crawford
10 X 10
Phaidon Press
Pamphlet Architecture 21: Situation Normal
Paul Lewis / Marc Tsurumaki
1995
1996
1997
1998
1999
2000

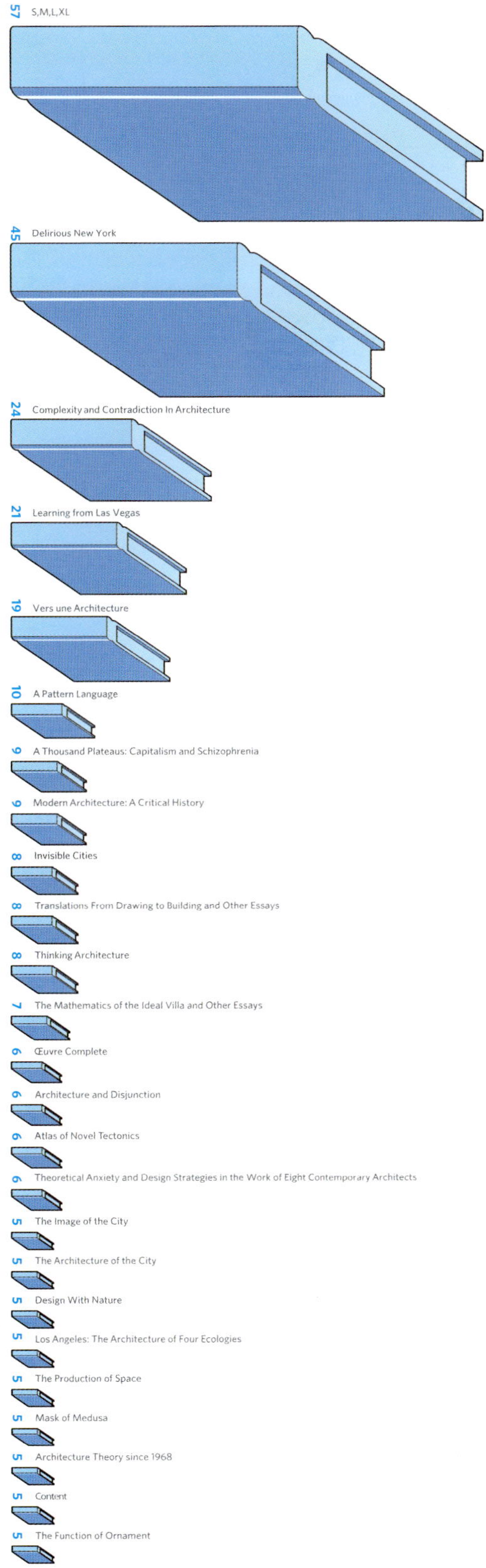

Most influential architecture books as listed by survey respondents. Graphic design: Kyle Jonasen.

32. Intersection of Santa Monica and San Diego freeways

the pursuit of that rural happiness was to lead to the postulation of a tamed arcadia, the ideal suburbia that never quite exists anywhere but is always just around the corner. The physical realization of this 'middle landscape'...was to involve two major 19th century phenomena powerful enough to smash a less potent vision - industrialization and democratization. In spite of Jefferson's suspicion of 'the mobs of great cities,' the dream that had been conceived as aristocratic and agrarian touched ground in most of the U.S. as an egalitarian vision based on advanced manufacturing techniques.

Peter Reyner Banham, "Frank Lloyd Wright's Wilderness Years," in *A Critic Writes*, Mary Banham, ed. (Berkeley and Los Angeles: University of California Press, 1996), 139.

THAT OBSCURE OBJECT
BRIAN TABOLT

The announcer had them off on the subject of housing developments, and the little Burke girl said she hated houses that all look alike--meaning a long row of identical 'development' houses. Zooey said they were 'nice.' He said it would be very nice to come home and be in the wrong house. To eat dinner with the wrong people by mistake, sleep in the wrong bed by mistake, and kiss everybody goodbye in the morning thinking they were your own family. He said he even wished everybody in the world looked exactly alike. He said you'd keep thinking everybody you met was your wife or your mother or father, and people would always be throwing their arms around each other wherever they went, and it would look 'very nice.' [1]

The scene is simultaneously comforting and terrifying. (Is it a coincidence that the girl's name is Burke...?)[2] Reyner Banham might also have identified it as a peculiarly *American* vision of equality - produced as it is by the twin forces of industrialization and democratization. The mechanical repetition of the 'development' houses, provides the environmental underpinning for a radical, willful, and collective abandonment of identity. In a hysterical embrace of equivalence, the fluid identity implicit in the industrialized environment is carried to its logical conclusion: a democratization so thorough that differences which remain no longer make a difference. Such a liberating (and disorienting) transformation would necessitate a continual process of forgetting. This is an operation that art historian Anton Ehrenzweig termed *dedifferentiation*: the conscious scattering of form, identity, and meaning.[3]

In the resulting condition of spectacular anonymity, the good gestalt of self is scattered and fragmented. To the extent that the boundaries which define identity evaporate, continuity is foregrounded in an 'oceanic' condition in which the contours between ourselves and space begin to dissolve, where "...space seems to constitute a will to devour."[4] Attributing characteristics, events, or stories to any one person would become meaningless. Under these circumstances, identity could no longer be understood as narrative, as the accumulation of past of events and actions. Instead, it could only be defined as an ongoing process of invention in a constant present. In such an anti-historical condition, inequality, and with it power, would be revealed as "nothing but an empty simulacrum and an isolated effect of perspective."[5]

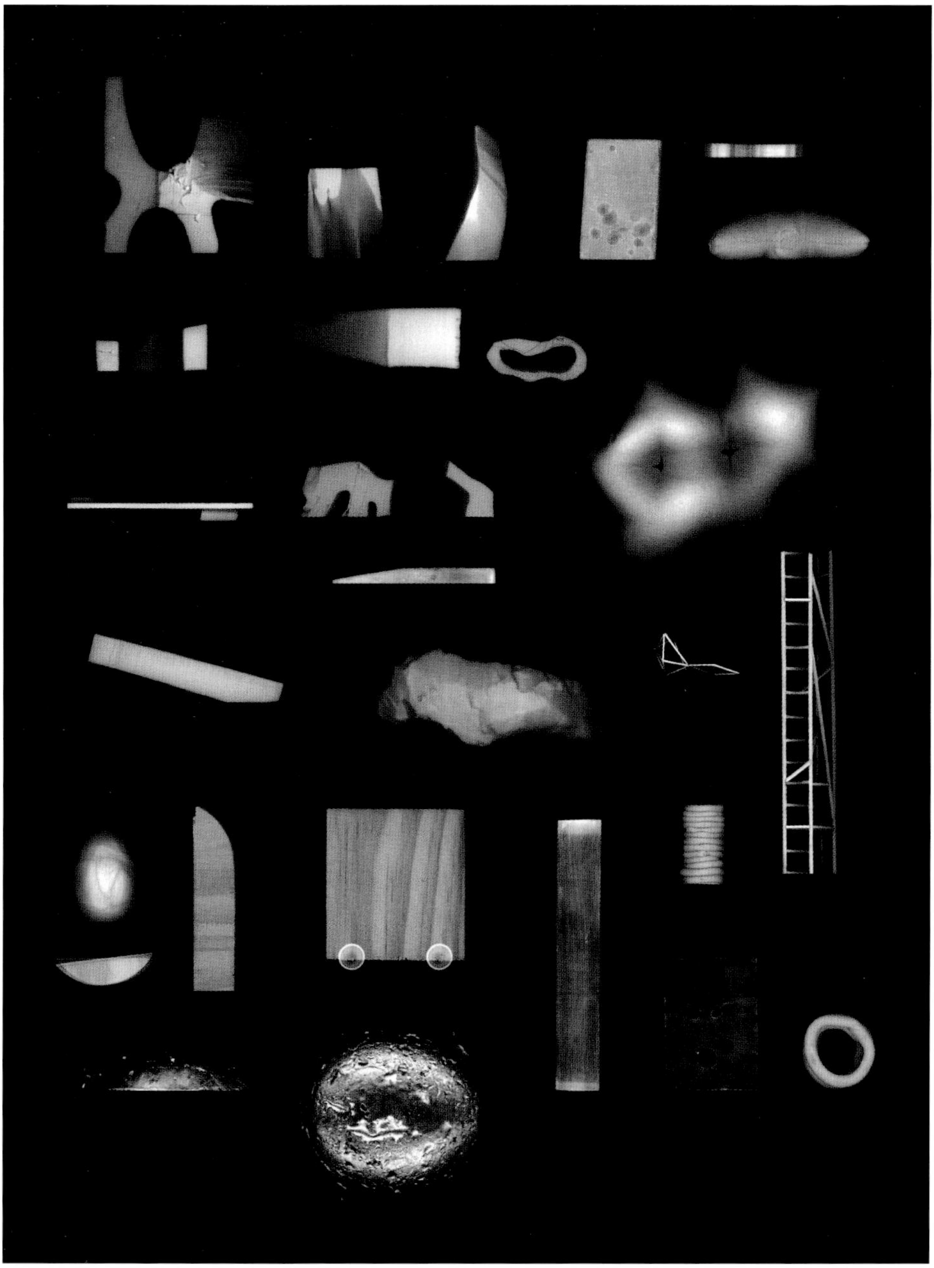

GRAY MATTER, 2010

(Pages 77-80) A collection of objects with no permanent relationship. They can easily occupy the concrete space of the page, or the urban field of a city like St. Louis, where the formless monumentality of the Mississippi River provides a perpetual instability.

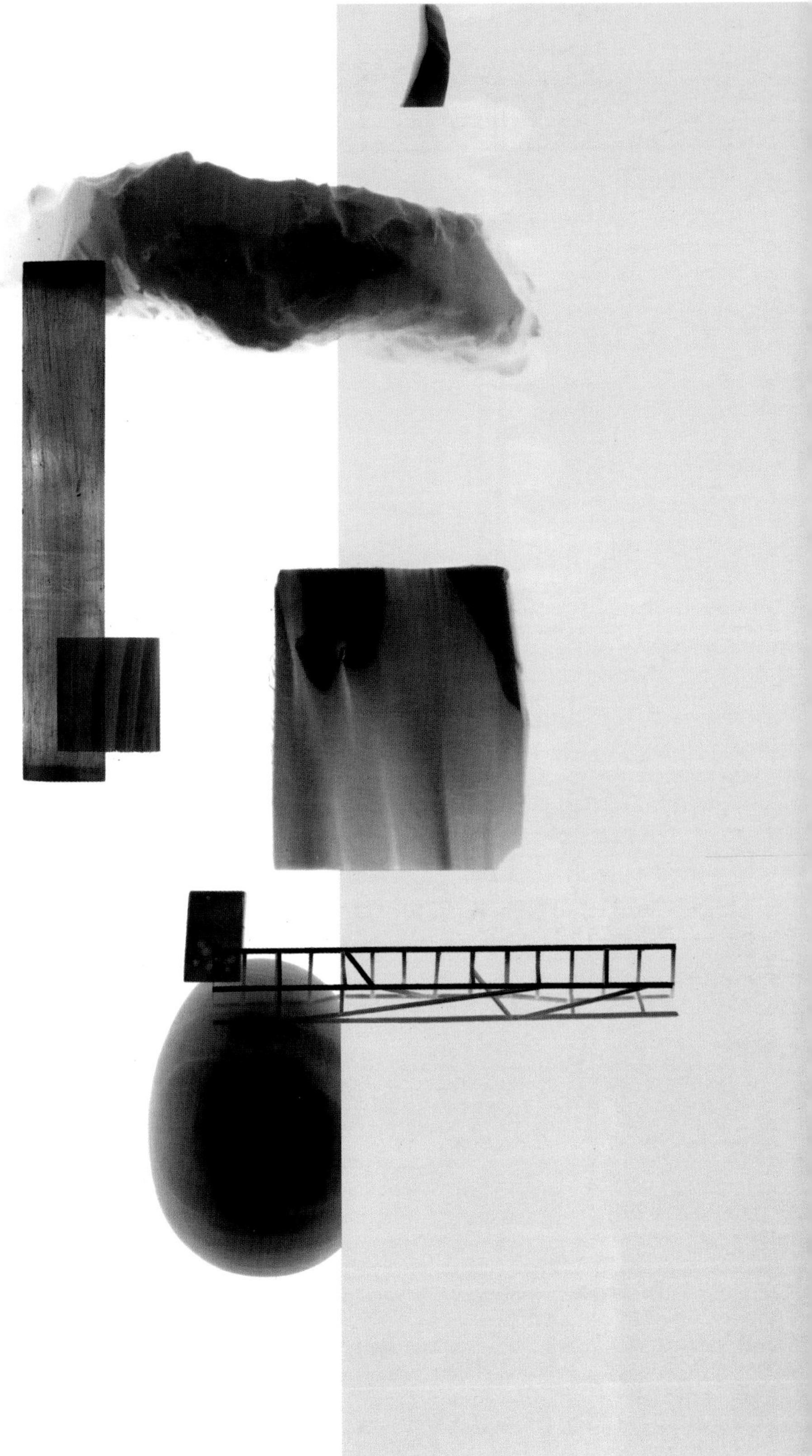

Perspective, of course, is a spatial structure that serves to establish rational relationships between objects through the objectification of space in which "...the great evolution from aggregate space to systematic space found its provisional conclusion."[6] Perspectival space is a representational tool, a technique for translating a three-dimensional scene onto two-dimensional surface, but its homogenizing rationalization of relationships now effects our perception of the concrete world as it collapses extremes of the universal and the arbitrary. This way of structuring space has become so naturalized that it's exposure as mere representational technique can be disturbing. For instance, Max Ernst's over-painting "The Master's Bedroom: It's Worth Spending A Night in It" of 1920 at first appears to be a simple painting of a room. In it, one can see some things: a table, a chest, a bed - but also a bear, a lamb, a whale, and a tree. The room is drawn as a simple one-point perspective. But the objects in the room stubbornly refuse to be organized by this rational container, refuse to fit into their "proper place". The absurd application of the perspectival structure, *after the fact,* reveals its organizing capacity as contingent, in fact fully reversing its familiar role. Here, perspective serves only to obfuscate rather than elucidate. A spatial structure finds itself, paradoxically, "out of place". The relationship between the objects in this field (once a page from an educational catalog) are, in turn, permanently destabilized. Rather than ground their meaning, to connect them with a universal reality, the vanishing lines of the floorboards only serve to "make them drift a little more than they seem to." In fact, one might say: "what should be suspected is their apparent unity; their collection is interesting insofar as some elements remain uncollected..."[7]

The concept of "over-painting" is interesting in and of itself - composition through covering, another kind of forgetting. In Ernst's case, it is also the injection of a foreign type of space between found objects. Ernst's use of perspective can be defined as a cloud- "...an unstable formation with no definite outline or color and yet that possesses the powers of a material in which any kind of figure may appear and then vanish."[8] Another territory of invention, a matrix actively engaged in suspending the specificity of relationships, of deferring the resolution of meaning and a reveling in the ecstasy of the concrete. Here, a political dimension emerges: "The masses, on the other hand, do not choose. They do not produce differences but a lack of differentiation - they retain a fascination for the medium which they prefer to the critical exigencies of the message. For fascination is not dependent on meaning, it is proportional to the disaffection of meaning."[9]

The projects included here also 'make things drift a little more than they seem to' - in this case operating on the various found urban contexts of Buffalo, St. Louis, Brooklyn, and Ostrava (in the Czech Republic.) Rather than regress towards an ideal urban projection, these works seek to produce processes of ongoing relationships existing in concrete, physical territories (both three and two dimensional). As a result, they can no longer be seen as things in themselves; they become things for us.[10] To this end, each project avoids introducing static patterns of use or structured narratives of development in order to experiment with creating conditions for the discovery of new logics of urban occupation. They therefore all contain some element which works to obscure (rather than insist on) the relationships between objects in order to necessitate invention and to prolong fascination.

FACTORY, BUFFALO 2009

(Pages 82-87) A speculative center for production and presentation, operating between the scales of big-boxes and single-family housing.

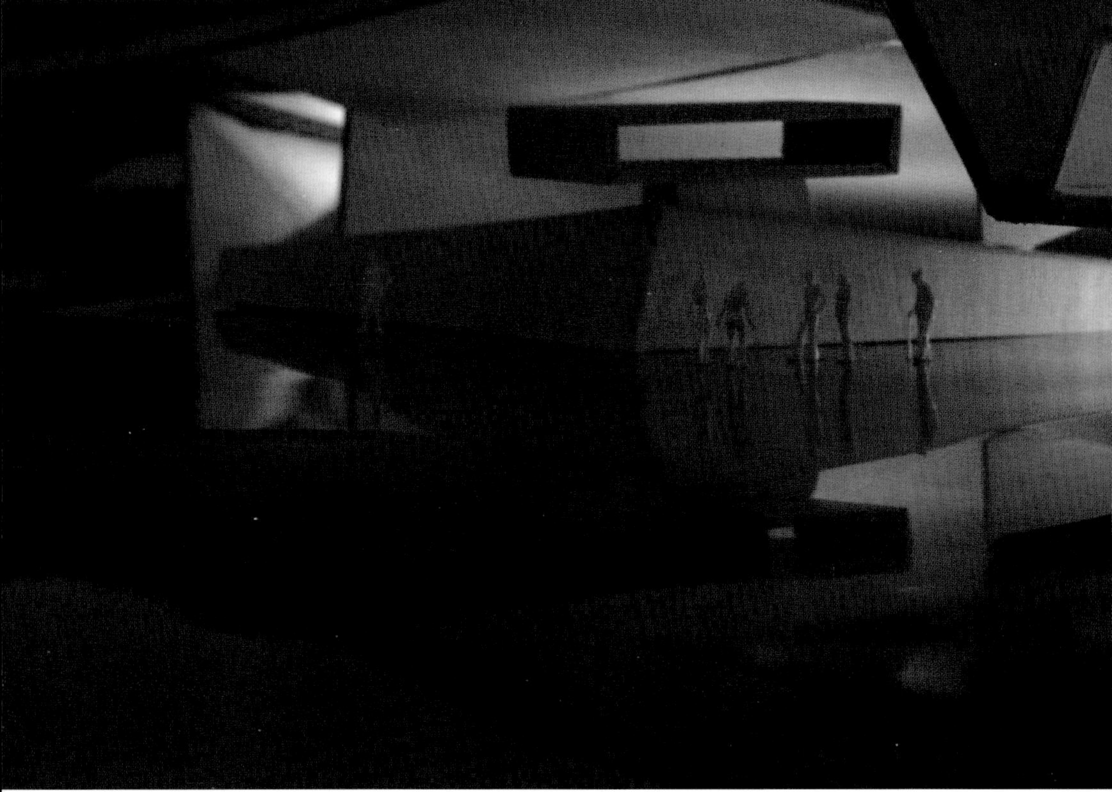

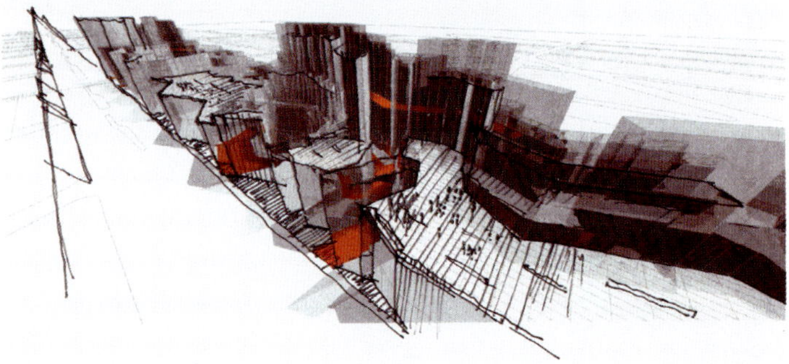

DOUBLED-UP URBANISM, BROOKLYN 2006

A proposal for an ongoing process for excessive construction; a model of proliferation that exploits the potentials of redundancy over efficiency.

WILDERNESS

+

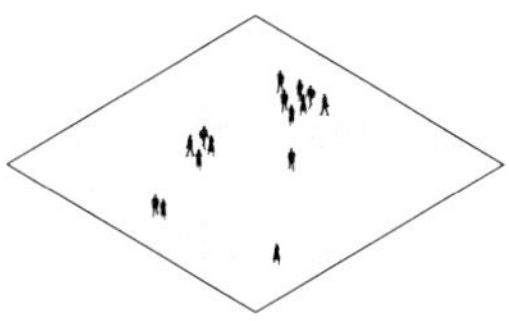

CLEARINGS

+

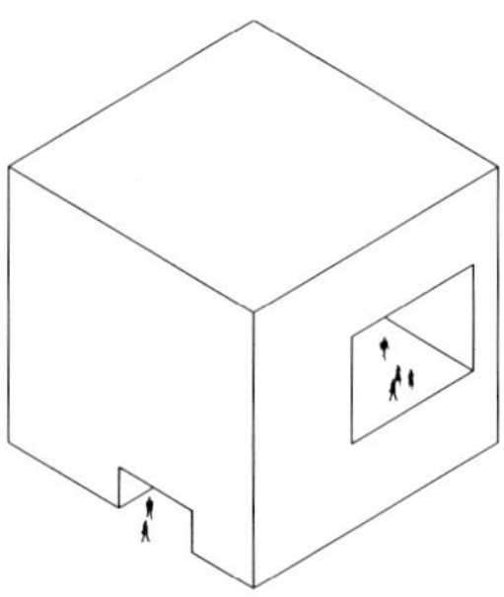

ROOMS

=

BLACK MEADOW, OSTRAVA 2010

With James Lowder and Peter Stec.

(Pages 90-93) We argue that cultural activity benefits from access to three distinct spatial conditions: First, a free, undifferentiated space in which exploration is allowed and encouraged. Second, a common ground where languages can be developed and ideas exchanged and stabilized.

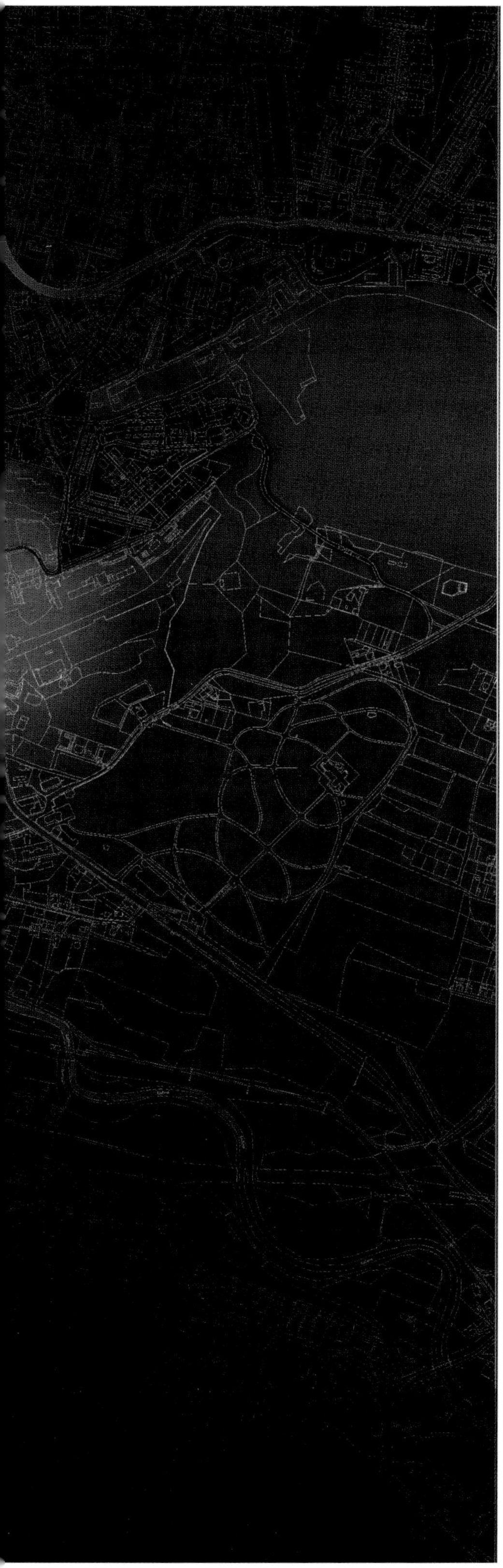

Third, recognizable building types such as the theater, concert hall, or museum, which allow for engagement with the past and the establishment of norms (if only to be challenged). We term the space of exploration and becoming "Wilderness", the space of provisional community "Clearings" and the most stable spaces dedicated to the harvesting of ripe cultural products "Rooms". We combine these conditions in a simple additive manner, acknowledging and encouraging the indefinite nature of their interactions

NOTES

1 J.D. Salinger, *Raise High the Roofbeam, Carpenters and Seymour, an introduction* (New York: Little, Brown, and Company, 1955), 68.

2 See Edmund Burke, *A Philosophical Enquiry* (Oxford: Oxford University Press, 1990).

3 Anton Ehrenzweig, *The Hidden Order of Art* (Berkeley: University of California Press,1967), 19.

4 See Roger Callois, "Mimcry and Legendary Psychansthenia" *The Edge of Surrealism: A Rodger Caillois Reader*, Claudine Frank, ed. (Durham: Duke University Press, 2003), 100.

5 Jean Baudrillard, *In the Shadow of the Silent Majorities* (Los Angles: Semiotext(e), 2007), 53.

6 Erwin Panofsky, *Perspective as Symbolic Form* (New York: Zone Books, 1997), 65.

7 Jean-Francois Lyotard, *Driftworks*. Roger Mckeon, ed. (Los Angles: Semiotext(e), 1984), 9-10.

8 Hubert Damisch, *A Theory of /Cloud/* (Stanford: Stanford University Press, 2002), 31.

9 Baudrillard, *In the Shadow of the Silent Majorities*, 58.

10 Paraphrased from Robert Smithson, *Robert Smithson: The Collected Writings*, Jack Flam, ed. (Berkeley: University of California Press,1996), 160.

CONTRIBUTORS

JONATHAN D SOLOMON
is an American architect based in Hong Kong, serving as the Acting Head of the Department of Architecture at the University of Hong Kong. He is a founding editor of 306090 Books, and has published several essays on the contemporary Asian city in the journal Log. In 2010, he co-curated the US Pavilion at the Venice Architecture Biennale, and in 2009, his design for Ooi Botos Gallery received two AIA awards. Solomon's proposal for converting a Bronx highway into a public park was published as the 26th volume of the acclaimed Pamphlet Architecture series from Princeton Architectural Press.

EVA FRANCH-GILABERT
is a Catalan architect, researcher, teacher, and founder of the Barcelona based OOAA (office of architectural affairs). In addition to being the Banham Fellow at Buffalo, she was later awarded the Wortham Fellowship at Rice University and since 2010 has served as the Director of Storefront for Art and Architecture in New York. She studied architecture at TU Delft, ETS Arquitectura Barcelona, and at Princeton University. Franch's work has been exhibited at the Center for Architecture in New York, Korean Institute of Architects in Daegu, FAD Barcelona, NAI Rotterdam, Shenzen Biennale of Architecture, among others. She lives and works in New York.

SERGIO LOPEZ-PIÑEIRO
is the founder of Holes of Matter. Currently an Assistant Professor in the Department of Architecture at the University at Buffalo, he has previously worked at NoMad (Madrid, 1998-2000) and at Foreign Office Architects (London, 2000-2002). López-Piñeiro graduated from ETS Arquitectura Madrid in 1998 and received his M. Arch. degree from Princeton University in 2004, where he was awarded the Suzanne Kolarik Underwood Prize.

MICHAEL KUBO
is pursuing a Ph.D. in the History, Theory, and Criticism of Architecture at MIT. His current work focuses on late modernist economies of production and the bureaucratic complex in which globalized, corporate architectural practices took shape in the decades after World War II. He has taught at Pratt Institute in New York, the University of Texas at Austin, and SUNY Buffalo.

BRIAN TABOLT
lives in Brooklyn. He received his Master of Architecture from Princeton University where he was a founding editor and co-designer of Pidgin Magazine. He holds a Bachelor of Science in Architecture with High Honors from the University of Virginia, where he was the recipient of the Z Society Edgar J Shannon Award for Design Excellence. In addition to teaching at the University at Buffalo, Tabolt has worked in the offices of SHoP Architects, Agrest & Gandelsonas, and Formwork Design and is currently a designer at Diller Scofidio + Renfro in New York.

MEHRDAD HADIGHI
is an architect and a Professor in the Department of Architecture at Buffalo. He served as Chair of Architecture between 2005 and 2010, when the five Banham fellows represented in this book were at Buffalo. Hadighi has been selected by the Architectural League of New York in their "Young Architects Forum" series; as one of "25 most intriguing, innovative and intrepid architects, from all over the world" by Wallpaper* magazine; and as one of "10 Young Firms Reshaping the Globe" by the Architectural Record magazine in their Design Vanguard issue. His work is the subject of a monograph by *Sharestan*, and his most recent work has been featured in *Conversions; Small Structures; Xs Green*; *Extensions and Renovations*; *House Plus*; and *Architecture In Detail*.